Twice Treasured Recipes

A Collection of Recipes with a Low Country Accent from Hilton Head Island

**Published by
The Bargain Box, Inc.**

546 William Hilton Parkway
Hilton Head Island, SC 29928

Pen and Ink Illustrations
Copyright Lois Petersen

Photographs
Copyright Skip Meachen

First Printing   5,000 copies   August, 2000

Printed in the USA by

WIMMER
The Wimmer Companies
Memphis
1-800-548-2537

We dedicate our cookbook in joyful memory to founding members: Billie Hack, Irene Wilkins and Mary Alice Williamson. And to the past, present and future volunteers and donors–the giving heart and soul of The Bargain Box.

Cookbook Committee 1999-2000

Editor and Design Chairman
Lyn Meachen

Illustrator and Book Design Advisor
Lois Petersen

Recipe Editors and Tasting Co-Chairmen
Bette Herbig & Roberta Mattka

Publicity and Marketing Co-Chairmen
Sally Kidd & Linda Vingelen

Treasurer and Bookkeeper
Connie Brooks

President and Cookbook Advisor
Betty Lewis

The recipes in this book reflect the many culinary and cultural roots of our diverse Island community. Some of our recipes are adventurous, others old-fashioned favorites. No claim is made as to the originality of

Twice Treasured Recipes.

However, the recipes have been tested, savored, adapted, and enjoyed. We hope y'all will enjoy them too!

Twice Treasured Recipes

The Bargain Box

A Collection of Recipes with a Low
Country Accent from Hilton Head Island

TWICE TREASURED RECIPES

Table of Contents

🌸 **Quick and Easy Recipes are designated with a camellia flower.**
🍃 **Memorable Menu Recipes are designated with a leaf.**

Introduction

The story of The Bargain Box and Hilton Head Island's modern history go hand in hand. The Bargain Box could not have existed for thirty-five years without the sharing, caring spirit of our Islanders—both native and new. The generosity of our community has created the unique entity, The Bargain Box.

Growth of The Bargain Box from the early days to the present is mirrored by the growth of Hilton Head Island. From a few thousand Island residents and three Bargain Box founders in 1965 it has grown to over 30,000 Island residents and over 300 Bargain Box volunteers in 2000.

Twice Treasured Recipes reflects the melding of native Islander cooking, and the influence of transplant Islanders from all over North America and in some cases the world. This in turn is a mirror of our larger mobile, global society and shows how much we have in common. It also shows the willingness to share treasured traditions: food after all is the hearth and heart of our families, and the basis of treasured memories.

A volunteer wished for a cookbook to share the treasured recipes served at our annual Bargain Box Volunteer potluck picnic. The wish grew, and it has become a celebration of thirty-five years of treasures we've shared--the gifts of time, expertise and, most importantly, giving hearts from a wide range of Islanders. It is another way for us to share our treasured Bargain Box with family, friends and visitors to Hilton Head Island.

The profits will be used to continue the valued work of The Bargain Box, making *Twice Treasured Recipes* a hope of financial benefits for future residents of the Low Country and the continued work of The Bargain Box and all the treasured charitable agencies it supports.

TWICE TREASURED RECIPES

The Bargain Box Story

Only about 500 people lived on Hilton Head until the late 1940's when a Georgia timber man named Fred Hack first saw its fine stand of pine and oak trees. With his arrival began Hilton Head Island's "modern" history.

The areas we know today as the Hilton Head, Palmetto Hall, Port Royal, Shipyard and Spanish Wells plantations, as well as Indigo Run, Long Cove, Wexford and other properties, were at various times purchased by Hack and his partners.

By 1965 the number of full time residents had grown to a few thousand. In June of that year Billie Hack (Fred's wife), Irene Wilkins and Mary Alice Williamson established The Bargain Box to sell donated items at bargain prices to raise money for "extras" for the First Presbyterian Church. Since then, both the Island and The Bargain Box have grown beyond the wildest dreams of their founders. The Island of Hilton Head has become an acclaimed international resort community, which has made a continuing effort to preserve its natural beauty and has become a model for communities up and down the eastern coast of the United States. The Bargain Box, less well known, but dearly loved by its many dedicated volunteers, donors and shoppers, has grown into a nondenominational charitable organization unlike any other on the Island. It serves more than 40 charitable agencies, and serves as a model organization for other communities—preserving families, homes and a feeling of good will in the Low Country.

For longtime as well as recent residents of the South Carolina Low Country, the Bargain Box is a convenient place to bring the clothes and collectibles left over after cleaning out closets and cupboards. After they remodel a home or villa, it's a number to call for a truck to pick up furniture or appliances. You might call The Bargain Box the Island's first recycling center.

For the customers of the nonprofit thrift shop, who come from all walks of life, it's a wonderland of treasures, worth waiting in line outside—sometimes for hours—to discover. It's a world of the affordable, the unexpected and the unusual, from an Oriental rug to a diamond bracelet to an antique butter churn. It's part serendipity and part pleasant habit that may become an addiction.

For more than 300 volunteers, The Bargain Box is a familiar environment, combining all of the above, along with the satisfaction of making a contribution to the community. To work there regularly—on the sales floor, in layaway, electrical repairs, or sorting and pricing—means you're part of a team that often feels like a family.

Island businesses also have contributed their time and resources to The Bargain Box, appraising books, jewelry or musical instruments, offering legal services or dry cleaning services and donating inventory items.

Most important, for many charitable agencies and churches of Beaufort County, The Bargain Box has often been the difference between success and failure. Hundreds of recipients have their own stories of fulfilled needs and appreciation for the cash donations which, over thirty-five years, have reached millions of dollars.

From all these different perspectives, The Bargain Box is a source of pride, accomplishment, friendship, and dedication to the Hilton Head community and the Low Country. What better way to celebrate the 35th anniversary of our founding than to share a bit of our homes and ourselves with you through treasured family recipes; thus preserving the gift of good food so often shared with loved ones.

About the Artists

Lois Petersen–Pen & Ink Illustrations

Lois volunteers in The Bargain Box Art Department and has been a featured artist at the Hilton Head Art League Gallery. Born in Park Ridge, Illinois, she studied at Northwestern University and the Art Institute of Chicago and was an interior designer at Marshall Fields in Chicago.

Lois began painting seriously when her children left the nest. She became hooked on watercolor and the "happy accidents" that can happen when you experiment with color.

In characterizing her work, Lois Petersen says, "My work is expressionistic. Some comes right out of my head. But I love what I see on Hilton Head."

Currently Mrs. Petersen's work can be seen at the Hilton Head Art League and the Palmetto Dunes Club and in private collections. While primarily known for her watercolors, Lois' love of the Low Country is amply expressed in the charming drawings she has created for *Twice Treasured Recipes*.

Skip Meachen–Photography

Island photographer since 1978, Skip has photographed countless weddings and family portraits for Islanders and visitors alike. His work has been printed in local and national publications and books including "Three Decades of Hilton Head Island Architecture." He also works with Island businesses and, when there's time, will artistically capture the beautiful treasures nature bestows on the Low Country. Some of these treasures are illustrated in his photographs featured throughout *Twice Treasured Recipes*.

TWICE TREASURED RECIPES

About the Cover

Twice Treasured Recipes' cover is a lovely scene of the Low Country. South Carolinians' beloved old moss covered oak was photographed one summer evening from the banks of Windmill Harbour on Hilton Head Island looking across the Intracoastal Waterway towards Bluffton, South Carolina.

About the Title Page and Drawings

Our title page is graced with an elegant drawing of a white heron under a sheltering oak limb draped with Spanish moss. The sheltering oak limb crowns the pages throughout *Twice Treasured Recipes*. The limb is combined with lovely illustrations of Carolina coastal scenes: children carrying a crab trap down the beach, a picturesque lighthouse, a sailboat racing before the wind or a pelican sitting on a post, that are often viewed by visitors and Islanders. Drawings of water lilies, stately egrets, squirrels, sought-after sweetgrass baskets, turtles basking on a log or a hammock inviting lazy afternoons, are sprinkled liberally throughout the cookbook for your enjoyment.

About the Table of Contents Photo

A peaceful view of The Bargain Box entrance when customers aren't queuing up to shop at the nonprofit second hand store for three hours on Monday, Wednesday, Friday and Saturdays. It's hard to believe, but true, that this unassuming little building is the fount of so much good for the Low Country and its people. Since 1965, The Bargain Box has been quietly earning and sharing millions of dollars with nonprofit charitable agencies throughout Beaufort County.

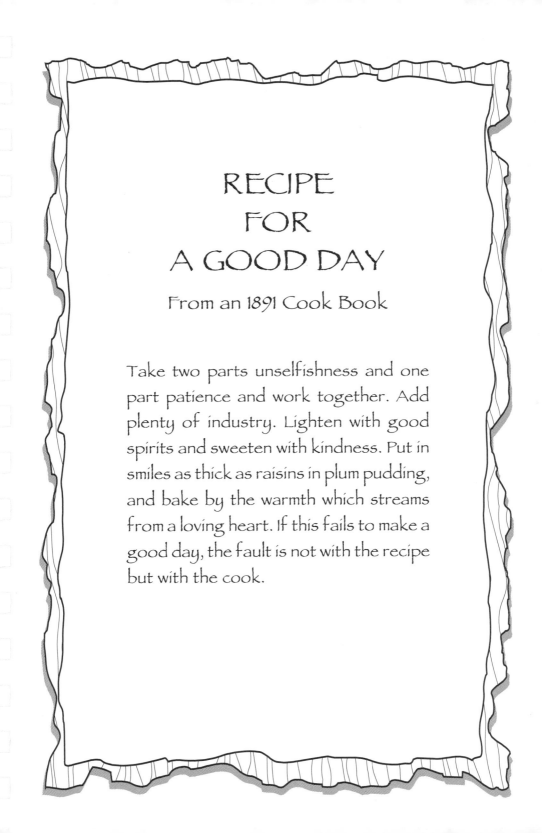

RECIPE
FOR
A GOOD DAY

From an 1891 Cook Book

Take two parts unselfishness and one part patience and work together. Add plenty of industry. Lighten with good spirits and sweeten with kindness. Put in smiles as thick as raisins in plum pudding, and bake by the warmth which streams from a loving heart. If this fails to make a good day, the fault is not with the recipe but with the cook.

Memorable Menus

Walk across a wooden bridge over a meandering stream on a late summer's afternoon and into the beginning of our Low Country recipe tour. We'll tantalize your thoughts and taste buds with choice meal ideas to serve your family and friends from *Twice Treasured Recipes*.

Here's a lovely view taken in Moss Creek Plantation. Step onto a wooden bridge leading to an island nature preserve on the other side of a tidal marsh and stream teeming with life. You can see the Spanish Moss hanging from an aged oak and almost hear sweet bird songs, buzzing insects and gentle breezes blowing through the marsh grasses.

Solar energy from long sunny days feeds the marsh grasses, which in turn feed fish, shrimp and shellfish that abound in Low Country marshes, ocean sounds and high seas. Alligators, ducks, geese, snowy egrets, blue herons, marsh wrens, swamp rabbits, occasional otter and other wildlife can be seen enjoying the endless edible feast nature provides.

You'll find many delicious recipes in *Memorable Menus* such as an old-fashioned Low Country Oyster Roast based on the treasures from the sea and marshes. The menus include tasty ways to prepare delectable fish and shellfish served with breads warm from the oven, savory side dishes, and sweet endings.

Read on to discover our twice treasured meal ideas . . .

Memorable
Menus

MEMORABLE MENUS

Memorable Menus Index

MEMORABLE MENUS

After Golf Supper

It's the end of the day—you and 19 or 23 friends and neighbors have just finished a fabulous 18 holes on one of Hilton Head's many memorable courses. Now the hungry horde is heading to your house. Here's a meal that can be prepared ahead and will satisfy the most ravenous guest.

Tee off with a delicious round of appetizers. *Glorified Vidalia Onions, Cheddar Delight* and *Okra Wagon Wheels* are guaranteed to take the edge off your guests' appetites and appeal to the most discriminating palate. Soar down the fairway with spicy *Tortilla Soup* partnered with *Bread Machine Focaccia,* a delectable flat bread flavored with herbs and olive oil. The crunch and refreshing taste of *Spinach Apple Toss* salad will win the trophy. And for a hole in one, you're sure to please the players with a rich, tasty *Carrot Cake.*

MEMORABLE MENUS

Boating Brunch

Whether sailing, cruising or at anchor get an early start on the sun and fun in the Low Country. Be prepared for your family's hunger pangs that are sure to arrive towards midday with this hearty brunch. Prepared ahead and served from your ample cooler you can keep the crew from mutiny and still join in the fun. Whet their appetites with a *Zesty Ham Ball* and healthy *Hummus.* Follow with a filling and delicious *Stuffed Italian Loaf* and a refreshing *Cold Cucumber Soup* perfect for the warm weather. The crew will make you captain when they're served *Melting Moments Cookies* and *Crème de Menthe Squares* which are sure to satisfy the hardiest sailor's sweet tooth.

MEMORABLE MENUS

Carolina Reunion

It's always a special occasion when families reunite to celebrate their heritage, renew old ties and meet the newest members. Hilton Head Island is often the meeting place of choice for these gatherings of the clans. Here's a noteworthy menu warranted to feed the largest assembly of kith and kin, leaving the youngest to the oldest looking forward to the next get-together.

MEMORABLE MENUS

Down-Home Family Dinner

A good, real down-home family dinner can renew and sustain the spirit. Each dish can be prepared ahead of time giving everyone an opportunity to enjoy the meal. Start out with *Piquant Stuffed Eggs* that will disappear before the plate has time to warm, while the aroma of *Chicken Cheese Lasagna* wafts deliciously through the house anticipated by all. Serve the lasagna with *One Hour Yeast Rolls* still warm and a colorful *Grecian Tossed Salad.* To complete the feast, the ultimate comfort food—served alone, à la mode or with a slice of cheese—*Grandma's Apple Pie.* A meal sure to inspire or bring back cozy thoughts and times.

MEMORABLE MENUS

Ladies To Luncheon

It's a lovely day, flowers are in bloom and well-dressed women are gathering in your home. You're sure to please them when you serve these tasteful dishes.

Totally Tea
Tips for the perfect pot of tea:

- Selecting good quality tea is the first step to the perfect pot of tea.
- Use cold water so tea is fresh and full of oxygen.
- If using an infuser or tea ball, don't fill to brim; tea leaves need room to expand.
- Heat the teapot by swirling hot water and then empty the pot. This helps maintain the water's boiling point and is crucial for proper brewing.
- When using loose tea, use 1 teaspoon per serving and one for the pot.

MEMORABLE MENUS

- Don't over boil the water; oxygen is lost and gives tea a muddy flavor.
- Average steeping time is 5 minutes—give the brew a stir, remove tea bags or infuser and savor this aromatic beverage.
- Serve tea with milk or cream, sugar cubes or honey, mint or very thinly sliced lemon.
- Instead of sugar, dissolve old-fashioned lemon drops, or if you prefer, hard mint or cinnamon candy. The candy melts quickly and is a pretty alternative in a sugar bowl.

Teas, like fine wines, reflect where they're grown; altitude, climate and soil all alter the flavor of the leaf. There are three basic types of tea; black, oolong and green teas. Black teas, Low Country favorites, are crushed and fermented before being dried. Oolong teas are partially fermented, steamed so the leaf is lighter brown when dried. Green teas are steamed, keeping their green color before being dried. Black teas are full bodied and delicious with milk and sugar when served hot and make good sweet iced tea when served cold. Iced tea is South Carolina's state beverage. Oolong teas are sparkling with an almost fruity flavor. You won't need sugar with your tea if you drink Jasmine tea or the lighter bodied varieties, like Formosa Oolong, which have their own natural sweetness. Green teas are delicate in color, flavor and aroma. The species from which tea is made is classified as Camellia sinensis. The common camellia is classified as Camellia japonica. Our *Quick and Easy Recipes* are marked with this lovely flower. In the winter the Low Country is gorgeously abloom with camellias of all colors and it is a good time to enjoy a fragrant cup of hot tea.

Tea is the world's most popular beverage except for water. South Carolina was the first place in the United States where tea was grown in 1799 and is the only state to ever have produced tea commercially. Tea continues to be produced commercially in the Low Country and you can find it for sale in many area grocery stores and specialty shops.

A woman is like a tea bag. It's only when she's in hot water that you realize how strong she is.

—Eleanor Roosevelt

MEMORABLE MENUS

Easy-as-Pie Low Country Social

The natural beauty, delicious weather and countless opportunities for fun on Hilton Head Island are a constant draw for visitors. Residents of the area, whether here for a short while or native, soon find their homes a popular vacation destination. Here's a delectable dinner that, prepared ahead of time, gives the host and hostess plenty of time to socialize.

MEMORABLE MENUS

4th of July Beach Picnic

It doesn't have to be the 4th of July to enjoy the beaches of Hilton Head Island, but what better excuse to fill your coolers and baskets with yummy vittles for an outdoor celebration. Everyone may head in a different direction when they first arrive, but sure as shootin' fireworks, they'll return to home base to relish these red, white and blue plate specials.

Halloween Treats

Here's the perfect table of treats to feed a swarm of famished small fry. Serve with platters of peanut butter or cheese spread stuffed celery, baby carrots and colorful sliced apples.

Create an eerie mood with simple games and prizes. Ghouls and boys will love guessing the number of black, yellow and orange jelly beans in a jar. Reward all your spooks with a favor from a prize pumpkin. Easy party favors are trick-or-treat bags filled with candy. Decorate with white sheets, stringy cobwebs and hanging spiders. Blindfold party goers and lead them through a feel and touch ghost house. To create a scary mood fill shoe boxes with "icky-feel" stuff like pudding, cooked cold noodles, and jelly. BOO!

Here are a few Low Country ghost stories to give a chill when the party heats up:

The Baynard Hall ruins are at the far end of Hilton Head Island in Sea Pines Plantation. Its remnants are thick tabby walls that can give one an eerie feeling. It's thought that it stood at the start of the American Revolution. According to tradition Baynard Hall was destroyed by the British when they roamed the Low Country. Long before the Island was a resort, old residents said that late at night mysterious men in strange dress with long bayonets swarmed over the tabby ruins and screams, carried on dark winds were heard for miles around. It's a fact that the Redcoats carried hundreds of slaves from coastal plantations to small barrier islands like Hilton Head and left them to die.

Another story that has come down to the present is that of the Baynard Bride. Of the many versions told, one is that soon after the house was built in 1830, William Baynard brought his beloved young wife to her new home on Hilton Head. When they were married, a vicious epidemic of yellow fever was raging along the South Carolina coast from Beaufort to Charleston. Hundreds, both black and white, were dying overnight.

MEMORABLE MENUS

The boat carrying the happy couple had just landed on the island when the new bride complained of a headache. Her face was flushed and when the groom gently took her hand he could feel it aflame with fever. Lifting her from the boat to the waiting carriage, the bride groom ordered the driver to make haste returning to Baynard Hall. Once home he allowed none but himself to nurse her. By the time they had reached the plantation the poor woman was delirious and as morning dawned the new bride had died.

Grief-stricken, the bridegroom buried his beloved in the family mausoleum at the Zion Cemetery. To this day, it is said that late on stormy nights the specter of a grand coach, with servants in scarlet livery, can be seen leaving the tabby ruins of Baynard Hall moving slowly as if following a hearse. Four sleek steeds draw the fine carriage and inside sits a deeply grieving man. As the coach approaches the Baynard mausoleum it evaporates from sight.

Another old tale is that years ago few folks wished to pass the Baynard mausoleum at night. Those who did claimed that on moonlit nights sobbing could be heard from an apparition in white standing near the door. The Baynards had been a wealthy family and there were stories that some family members were buried with valuable jewelry. The tomb was unmolested; even the Union soldiers stationed on Hilton Head Island during the Civil War kept their distance. It may be that the spirit protected the family's resting place. During World War II, the spirit failed to strike fear, the mausoleum was entered, coffins opened and left on the ground. The mausoleum stands empty today on William Hilton Parkway in the Zion Cemetery.

MEMORABLE MENUS

Old-Fashioned Oyster Roast

Nothing says "Low Country" like an old-fashioned oyster roast. So come on over y'all and stay a while, y'hear.

*Roasted Oysters (see instructions below)

Cocktail Sauce 263

Lemon Cocktail Sauce 263

Shrimp Salad Bake 144

Vidalia Onion Supper Bread 52

Marinated Broccoli 122

Carrot Salad 116

Baked Cheese Grits 87

Sweet Potato Casserole 199

Hoppin' John (especially if the roast is on New Year's Day) 92

Pecan Pumpkin Pie 252

Turtle Bars 227

Carolina Iced Tea 81

*Before digging your pit for the oyster roast, choose a nice sunny spot near the hose. Get a sheet of heavy roofing tin about 4x4 feet so it will fit securely over concrete blocks or bricks placed around the pit. Clear the immediate area around the pit of any flammable debris. Choose single oysters and have them washed and thoroughly scrubbed. This can be done the day before if the nights are cool. Start a good blaze before the guests arrive, allowing it to burn down to very hot coals. When the guests appear and the fire's ready, shovel the oysters onto the metal sheet and cover them with clean croaker sacks (burlap sacking) that have been soaked in cold water. (A flat metal shovel similar to a snow shovel works best.) The oysters are ready to eat when the shells begin to pop open. Shovel them onto a big old table and stand back while folks dig in. Gloves or heavy rags should be provided for all your guests as well as oyster knives. Keep plenty of big trash cans near the table so folks can shuck the shells. Bowls of melted butter, lemon juice and butter, *Cocktail Sauce, Lemon Cocktail Sauce,* sliced lemons and Tabasco sauce are placed on the table with the oysters. Pry the oysters open at the hinge, NOT the lip and enjoy. This is the start of a scrumptious Low Country feast.

Appealing Appetizers

It's always inviting to start at the beginning. We'll help you appeal to your loved one's senses with tantalizing tidbits from *Twice Treasured Recipes*.

The photo for *Appealing Appetizers* shows a mirrored reflection of an egret standing motionless. The egret is waiting to stab its lightning quick yellow bill into the water for an appetizer, and is often seen in the green twilight hour.

These long-plumed waders are found along ponds, rice fields, streams and fresh water marshes in the Low Country together with their close relatives the Blue Herons. The egret is larger than any other white heron except the Great White and holds its neck in a sinewy loose "S" curve when wading or in flight. They're seen gracefully gliding to land to feed on favorite snacks of crabs, snails, minnows and frogs—all considered edible in more than one culinary circle. If disturbed, the egret slowly takes flight, tucking up black legs against its torso for balance, and leisurely beating large snowy wings until aloft.

In this section you will find appealing appetizers that are served by Islanders for friends to nibble while enjoying the splendors nature bestows on Hilton Head; or for your family while quietly sitting on the screened porch overlooking nature's green twilight hour, before dinner's ready.

Appealing
Appetizers

Appealing Appetizers

🌸**Quick and Easy Recipes are designated with a camellia flower.**

🍃 **Memorable Menu Recipes are designated with a leaf.**

Pecan-Blue Cheesecake

2 tablespoons butter or margarine	¼ cup all-purpose flour
1 cup crushed herb-seasoned stuffing mix	1 cup sour cream
	¼ cup picante sauce
2 (8-ounce) packages cream cheese, softened	¼ teaspoon salt
	½ cup chopped green onions
8 ounces blue cheese, crumbled	½ cup chopped pecans
	Garnishes: tomato rose, fresh parsley sprigs
3 large eggs, lightly beaten	

Spread butter on bottom and sides of an 8-inch springform pan. Sprinkle stuffing mix on bottom and sides; set aside. Combine cream cheese, blue cheese, eggs, flour, salt, picante sauce and sour cream in a large bowl. Fold in onion. Pour mixture into prepared pan and sprinkle with pecans. Bake at 325 degrees for 1 hour or until a knife inserted into the center comes out clean. Cover and chill 8 hours or overnight. Carefully remove sides of springform pan. Garnish with tomato rose surrounded by parsley. Serve at room temperature with crackers.

Yield: 20 to 25 servings

Cheese can be sliced thinner with a dull knife rather than a sharp one. If the knife gets sticky, fold wax paper over the blade for cleaner cuts. Hard cheese cuts easier with a warm knife.

 Brie with Kahlúa

¾ cup finely chopped pecans	3 tablespoons brown sugar
¼ cup Kahlúa	1 (14-ounce) whole Brie

Spread pecans evenly in a 9-inch glass pie plate. Microwave at HIGH for 4 to 6 minutes, stirring every 2 minutes, until toasted. Combine pecans, Kahlúa and brown sugar in a small bowl. Microwave at HIGH until the brown sugar is dissolved. Stir until well blended. Remove rind from top of Brie and discard. Place Brie on microwavable plate; top with pecan mixture. Microwave, uncovered, at HIGH 1½ to 2 minutes or until Brie is softened, giving dish a ½ turn after 1 minute. Be sure to watch carefully to avoid overheating. Brie should be softened but not melted. Serve Brie with crackers.

Yield: 12 servings

Chinese Meatballs

1 pound lean ground beef	¼ cup chili sauce
½ cup seasoned dry bread crumbs	1 tablespoon Worcestershire sauce
½ cup evaporated milk	1 teaspoon salt
½ cup finely chopped onion	½ teaspoon pepper

Sauce:

1 (12-ounce) jar chili sauce	1-2 teaspoons hot Chinese mustard
1 (10-ounce) jar apple jelly	

Combine beef, bread crumbs and milk in a large bowl. Stir in onion, chili sauce, Worcestershire, salt and pepper, mixing lightly. Shape mixture into 1-inch balls (about the size of a walnut); place in a 13 x 9 x 2-inch baking dish. Bake at 400 degrees for 12 to 15 minutes. Combine remaining jar of chili sauce, apple jelly and mustard in a large saucepan over medium heat, stirring constantly. Add meatballs, stirring until coated. Cook for 15 minutes. Serve hot in a chafing dish or crock pot.

Yield: 5 dozen

Cheese Wiches  ✓

*Guests will love these dainty and delicious appetizers
for any occasion. Serve with apéritifs, coffee and hot or iced tea.*

½ cup unsalted butter, softened
2 (5-ounce) jars sharp process
   cheese spread
½ teaspoon onion powder
¾ teaspoon Worcestershire
   sauce

¾ teaspoon dill weed
½ teaspoon hot pepper sauce
1 large loaf thinly sliced white
   sandwich bread

Combine butter and cheese in the container of a food processor, pulsing until blended. Add onion powder, Worcestershire, dill weed and hot pepper sauce; pulse until well blended. Cut crusts from bread and spread 3 slices with cheese mixture. Stack the three slices and cut into 9 equal squares; place on a baking sheet. Repeat with remaining cheese mixture and bread. (You may freeze the sandwiches on baking sheets, then remove and store in plastic freeze bags.) Bake at 350 degrees for 12 minutes.

Yield: about 7 ½ dozen

Cheddar Delight

1 bunch green onions, sliced
1 ½ cups (6 ounces) shredded
   white cheddar cheese
1 cup chopped ripe olives
½ cup mayonnaise

½ teaspoon curry powder
½ scant teaspoon salt
12 English muffins, split and
   toasted

Combine onion, cheese and olives in a mixing bowl. Combine mayonnaise, curry powder and salt; stir into onion mixture. Spread mixture on toasted muffin halves and cut into 3 triangles. Place triangles on a baking sheet. Cover and freeze until ready to serve. Bake at 350 degrees for 8 to 10 minutes or until hot.

Yield: 6 dozen

Christmas Snowball

1 (8-ounce) package cream cheese, softened
1 (8-ounce) can crushed pineapple, well drained
¼ (9-ounce) jar chutney, finely chopped
1 (7-ounce) package flaked coconut, finely chopped
1 (10-ounce) package fresh spinach
1 pint fresh strawberries

Combine cream cheese, pineapple and chutney in a medium bowl, blending well. Shape mixture into a ball. Roll ball in coconut; cover and refrigerate 4 to 6 hours. Place spinach leaves on a serving plate; place ball in center of spinach. Garnish with strawberries, placing one on top of ball. Serve with crackers in a holiday dish.

Yield: 8 to 10 servings

Note: Chopped pecans may be substituted for coconut.

 # Date-Bacon Appetizers

Bacon, each slice cut into 4 pieces
Dates
½ cup firmly packed light brown sugar
¼ cup red wine
1 teaspoon prepared mustard

Wrap bacon around dates and secure with a toothpick. Place in a large, shallow dish. Combine brown sugar, wine and mustard; pour mixture over dates, tossing to coat. Marinate dates for 20 minutes; drain and place on a baking sheet. Bake at 350 to 400 degrees for 10 to 15 minutes. Serve warm.

Yield: 2 to 3 dates per serving

🍃 *Corned Beef Pâté*

1	(12-ounce) can corned beef	½	cup minced onion
1	(8-ounce) package braunschweiger	1	tablespoon vinegar
½	cup mayonnaise	1	tablespoon Dijon mustard

Flake corned beef with a fork and spoon into a bowl. Stir in braunschweiger, mayonnaise, onion, vinegar and mustard. Place ½ cup of mixture into a blender; process at medium speed until smooth. Repeat with remaining mixture. Spoon mixture into a 3½-cup mold or bowl; cover and chill at least 24 hours. Turn pâté out onto a serving plate. Serve with cocktail rye bread or rye crackers.

Yield: 3½ cups

🍃 *Curried Chicken Bites*

1	(8-ounce) package cream cheese, softened	1½	cups toasted almonds
3	tablespoons mayonnaise	3	tablespoons chutney
2	cups cooked chicken, finely chopped	2	teaspoons curry powder
		1	teaspoon salt
			Flaked coconut

Combine cream cheese and mayonnaise in a large bowl, blending well. Place chicken, almonds and chutney in a food processor. Process until finely chopped. Stir chicken mixture into cream cheese mixture. Stir in curry powder and salt. Cover and refrigerate 8 hours or overnight. Roll chicken mixture into 1-inch balls. Roll balls in flaked coconut. Cover and refrigerate until ready to serve.

Yield: 3 to 3½ dozen

Zesty Ham Ball

2	(4 ½-ounce) cans deviled ham		Hot pepper sauce
3	tablespoons chopped pimiento-stuffed olives	1	(3-ounce) package cream cheese, softened
1	tablespoon prepared mustard	2	teaspoons milk

Combine ham, olives and mustard in a medium bowl, blending well. Stir in hot pepper sauce, to taste. Shape ham mixture into a ball. Cover and refrigerate until firm. Combine cream cheese and milk; spread over ball. Refrigerate until ready to serve. Serve with crackers.

Yield: 10 to 12 servings

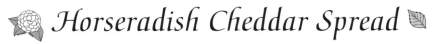

Horseradish Cheddar Spread

Place this zesty spread in decorative containers for excellent small gifts. Cheeses should be served at room temperature—approximately 70 degrees.

2	(8-ounce) packages sharp cheddar cheese, shredded	⅓	cup prepared horseradish
2	(8-ounce) packages cream cheese, softened	¼	cup white Worcestershire sauce
		2	teaspoons dry mustard

Combine cheddar cheese, cream cheese, horseradish, Worcestershire sauce and mustard in a food processor. Process until mixture is well blended and smooth. Place spread in five 1-cup containers.

Yield: 5 containers

APPEALING APPETIZERS

 *Okra Wagon Wheels*

*Protect silver trays from the acid in food by
covering the tray with a layer of leafy green lettuce.*

1   (16-ounce) jar pickled okra
1   pound turkey pastrami

1   (8-ounce) package cream
    cheese, softened

Drain okra; cut off ends and dry on paper towels. Cut pastrami to length of okra. Spread cream cheese thinly on pastrami. Place okra on top of cream cheese and roll, jelly-roll style. Place rolls seam side down in a food storage container; cover and refrigerate 8 hours or overnight. To serve, cut each roll into ¼-inch slices. Place slices on a serving dish, cut side up, to resemble wagon wheels.

Yield: approximately 4 dozen

Tortellini in Herb-Garlic Dressing

1   (8-ounce) package of fresh or
    frozen cheese tortellini
⅓   cup imported extra-virgin
    olive oil
¼   cup red wine vinegar
1   clove garlic, minced
1   tablespoon Dijon mustard
    Salt
    White pepper

8   leaves fresh basil, finely
    chopped or 2 teaspoons
    dried
2   tablespoons chopped fresh
    parsley
4   green onions, finely chopped
½   cup finely grated Parmesan
    cheese

Cook tortellini in boiling salted water until tender but still firm; drain and rinse with cold water. Place tortellini in serving bowl. Beat oil and vinegar until well blended. Stir in garlic and mustard; season to taste with salt and pepper. Pour mixture over tortellini, tossing gently to coat. Add basil, parsley and green onion; toss gently. Sprinkle with cheese. Serve chilled with skewers.

Yield: 8 to 10 appetizer servings

APPEALING APPETIZERS

Stuffed Belgian Endive

16-20 endive leaves	Alfalfa sprouts
Herbed cream cheese	Ripe olives

Spread or pipe endive leaves with 1 tablespoon cream cheese. Arrange leaves in a circular pattern on a large, round serving platter. Place alfalfa sprouts in center and fill with ripe olives. Recipe can be made ahead; cover and chill until ready to serve.

Yield: 12 to 16 servings

Piquant Stuffed Eggs

8	hard-cooked eggs, halved	½	teaspoon minced onion
3	slices crisp cooked bacon, finely chopped	¼	teaspoon salt
			Pinch paprika
2	tablespoons chili sauce		Mayonnaise
1	teaspoon tarragon vinegar		

Mash yolks in a medium bowl. Stir in bacon, chili sauce, vinegar, onion, salt, paprika and enough mayonnaise to make a smooth paste. Stuff egg whites with mixture. Cover and refrigerate until ready to serve. These eggs are good served on toast with white sauce.

Yield: 16 halves

Deviled Eggs Tips—Always start with fresh eggs and cold water; bring eggs and water to boil and simmer for 20 minutes. While the eggs are cooking stir them a few times so the yolk will stay in the center. When eggs are done cooking fill pan with cold water and ice cubes. Once eggs are chilled they should be perfect for peeling and slicing in half.

Holiday Squares Florentine ✓

2	(10-ounce) packages frozen chopped spinach, thawed	½	cup minced green onions
1	(10¾-ounce) can cream of mushroom soup	½	cup chopped toasted walnuts
4	large eggs, lightly beaten	¼	cup grated Parmesan cheese
1	cup shredded Swiss cheese	1	(8-ounce) package refrigerated crescent rolls

Drain spinach thoroughly; mince and place in a large mixing bowl. Stir in soup, eggs, Swiss cheese, green onion, walnuts and Parmesan cheese. Unroll crescent rolls but do not separate. Place crescent dough in the bottom of a greased 13 x 9 x 2-inch baking dish. Press seams together. Spread spinach mixture over dough. Bake at 350 degrees for 40 minutes or until knife inserted in center comes out clean. Cut into 1-inch pieces.

Yield: approximately 4 dozen

Salmon Ball

1	(8-ounce) package cream cheese, softened	¼	teaspoon liquid smoke
1	tablespoon lemon juice	¼	teaspoon salt
2-3	teaspoons grated onion	1	cup canned or cooked salmon, drained and flaked
1	teaspoon prepared horseradish	½	cup chopped pecans or chopped fresh parsley

Combine cream cheese, lemon juice, onion, horseradish, liquid smoke and salt in a mixing bowl. Fold in salmon. Shape salmon mixture into 1 or 2 balls and roll in chopped pecans or parsley. Serve with crackers. Recipe may be made ahead and frozen.

Yield: 12 to 15 servings

Sauerkraut Meatballs

These flavorful meatballs are a good addition to any cocktail buffet.

2	pounds lean ground beef	1	(1 ¾-ounce) package onion soup mix
1	pound mild sausage		
1	cup dry bread crumbs	3	large eggs, lightly beaten

Sauce:

1	(15-ounce) bottle chili sauce	2	cups water
1	(15-ounce) can sauerkraut, drained	¾	cup firmly packed light brown sugar
1	(15-ounce) can whole cranberry sauce		

Combine beef, sausage, bread crumbs, soup mix and eggs in a large bowl. Shape mixture into 1-inch balls (about the size of a walnut). Place in a 13 x 9 x 2-inch baking pan. Combine chili sauce, sauerkraut, cranberry sauce, water and brown sugar in a large saucepan over medium heat. Cook until mixture is well blended and sugar is melted. Pour sauce over meatballs. Bake at 350 degrees for 1 ½ hours. A good addition to a cocktail buffet.

Yield: 4 dozen

✓ Hot Artichoke Dip

1	(14-ounce) can artichoke hearts, rinsed and drained	1	cup mayonnaise
		1	cup grated Parmesan cheese

Dice artichoke hearts and mash with a fork in a mixing bowl. Stir in mayonnaise and Parmesan cheese. Spoon mixture into a lightly greased 1-quart baking dish. Bake at 350 degrees for 20 minutes or until hot and bubbly. Serve with crackers.

Yield: 6 to 8 servings

Hot Clam Dip

1   (1-pound) loaf round bread
1   (8-ounce) package cream
      cheese, softened

1   (6 ½-ounce) can minced clams

Hollow out the round loaf of bread leaving a 1-inch shell. Cut the removed pieces of bread into cubes; set aside. Combine cream cheese and clams in a small saucepan over low heat. Cook until mixture is warm. Spoon clam mixture into center of bread. To eat, dip the cubes into the clam dip. The outside crust can be broken later into pieces and eaten.

Yield: 10 to 12 servings

Caviar Pie

2   (8-ounce) packages cream
      cheese, softened
1   (3-ounce) package cream
      cheese, softened
1   cup mayonnaise
1   small onion, grated

1   tablespoon Worcestershire
      sauce
1   tablespoon lemon juice
      Dash hot pepper sauce
2   (3 ½-ounce) jars caviar
4   hard-cooked eggs, chopped
1   cup chopped fresh parsley

Combine cream cheese, mayonnaise, onion, Worcestershire sauce, lemon juice and hot sauce in a large bowl, stirring until well blended. Spoon mixture into a 9-inch pie plate. Spread caviar on top of pie. Combine eggs and parsley and sprinkle over caviar. Cover and refrigerate until ready to serve. Serve with crackers.

Yield: 10 to 12 servings

Tomato Cheese Dip

1 pound process cheese loaf	1 (10-ounce) can diced tomatoes and green chiles

Combine cheese and tomatoes in a medium saucepan over low heat. Cook, stirring constantly, until cheese is melted. You can also cook recipe in the microwave for 5 minutes, stirring every 1 minute until cheese is melted. Serve with Tortilla chips.

Yield: 10 to 12 servings

Swiss Almond Spread

1 (8-ounce) package light cream cheese, softened	⅓ cup light mayonnaise or salad dressing
1½ cups shredded Swiss cheese	2 tablespoons chopped green onions
⅓ cup toasted sliced almonds	

Combine cream cheese, Swiss cheese, almonds, mayonnaise and green onion in a bowl, mixing well. Spread mixture into a 9-inch pie plate. Bake at 350 degrees for 12 minutes. Serve with vegetables and pita chips.

Yield: 8 to 10 servings

 Cheeses should be served at room temperature (approximately 70 degrees).

Low Country Crab Dip

1 (8-ounce) package cream cheese, softened	½ teaspoon prepared horseradish
6-7 ounces crabmeat, drained	¼ teaspoon salt
2 tablespoons chopped onion	Dash pepper
1 tablespoon milk	Toasted slivered almonds (optional)

Combine cream cheese, crabmeat, onion, milk, horseradish, salt and pepper in a bowl. Spoon into a lightly greased baking dish. Top with almonds, if desired. Bake at 375 degrees for 15 minutes. Serve on crackers.

Yield: 8 to 10 servings

Hummus

2 cloves garlic	1 tablespoon chopped fresh parsley
1 (19-ounce) can chickpeas, rinsed and drained	1 teaspoon lemon-pepper seasoning
3 lemons	1 teaspoon dried dill weed
½ cup olive oil	

Drop garlic into food processor with the motor running; process until minced. Add chickpeas; process until pureed. Add grated peel from lemons. Cut lemons in half and squeeze juice into the food processor. Add oil, parsley, lemon-pepper and dill weed. Process until smooth and well blended. Serve with toasted pita pieces and raw vegetables.

Yield: 1 ½ cups

 Crab-Cheese Dip

1 (8-ounce) package process cheese loaf, cubed	Dash Worcestershire sauce
½ cup butter	Hot pepper sauce
1 (6 ½-ounce) can crabmeat, drained and flaked	Salt
	Pepper

Combine cheese and butter in a medium saucepan over low heat. Cook until melted and well blended. Stir in crab, Worcestershire sauce, hot pepper sauce, salt and pepper. Serve warm with round buttery crackers.

Yield: 6 to 8 servings

Spinach Balls

4 (10-ounce) packages frozen chopped spinach, thawed	2 large onions, chopped
1 (16-ounce) package herb-seasoned stuffing mix	½ cup butter, melted
	½ cup grated Parmesan cheese
6 large eggs, lightly beaten	1 tablespoon garlic salt
	1 tablespoon pepper

Cook spinach according to package directions; drain. Combine spinach, stuffing mix, eggs, onion, butter, Parmesan cheese, garlic salt and pepper in a large bowl. Roll into balls and place on a lightly greased baking pan. Bake at 350 degrees for 20 minutes.

Yield: 4 to 5 dozen

 # Glorified Vidalia Onions

5-6 Vidalia onions, finely chopped   ½ cup apple cider vinegar
2   cups water   ½ cup mayonnaise
1   cup sugar   1 teaspoon celery salt

Combine onions, water, sugar and vinegar in a large bowl. Cover and refrigerate for 2 to 4 hours. Drain in a colander for 45 minutes and pat dry. Combine onions, mayonnaise and salt and place in a serving dish. Serve with crackers.

Yield: 12 servings

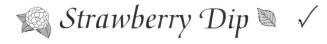 # Strawberry Dip

4   heaping tablespoons sour   2 tablespoons orange curaçao
    cream   1 tablespoon orange liqueur
4   heaping tablespoons frozen   ½ tablespoon dark rum
    non-dairy topping, thawed   Strawberries
2   tablespoons light brown
    sugar

Beat together sour cream and topping at medium speed with an electric mixer until fluffy. Beat in brown sugar, orange curaçao, orange liqueur and rum. Spoon into a serving bowl and serve with strawberries.

Yield: 4 servings

Breads & Brunch

Rise and take a shine to tasty ways to break bread or a fast. The sun is shining and the smell of bread wafts through the house. What a delicious start to the day. *Twice Treasured Recipes* serves up mouthwatering recipes for *Breads & Brunch* for those days when you feel like sleeping in or eating late.

The *Breads & Brunch* scene shows Sea Oats in Port Royal Plantation waving in a beach breeze. This hearty grass is not only beautiful, but plays an important part in the Low Country's beaches. Their roots stabilize sand dunes and create a place for other plants to colonize. A six-inch plant may have roots five feet long. The long root system helps dunes hold their own against erosion, and the Sea Oat plant traps windblown sand, encouraging growth of the sand dunes.

In the summer the heavy golden plumes of "oats" look similar to those oats we grow for food, hence the name Sea Oats. At the end of the summer when the plumes have matured, seeds are dispersed on the Island winds along our white sand beaches.

In this section you will find bountiful breads and satisfying brunches that are sure to fill the appetites and memories of your cherished ones.

Breads
& Brunch

Breads & Brunch

Breads

Brunch

🌸**Quick and Easy Recipes are designated with a camellia flower.**

🍃 **Memorable Menu Recipes are designated with a leaf.**

Old Mill Oatmeal Bread

Years ago when traveling through Georgia, we spotted an old mill. I wanted to buy some grits and at the same time show the children a working mill. While there, a woman (another tourist) asked if I would like some bread recipes. She took my address and in a few weeks, sent me several recipes. The Oatmeal Bread was my favorite. I have used the recipe many times and everyone loves it. It is especially good toasted.

½ cup warm water (105 to 115 degrees)	2 cups boiling water
3 (¼-ounce) envelope active dry yeast	2 cups cold water
2 cups oats	½ cup wheat germ
1 cup firmly packed light brown sugar	2 cups whole wheat flour
¾ cup vegetable oil	7-8 cups unbleached all-purpose flour
¼ cup molasses or cane syrup	Nuts (optional)
2 teaspoons salt	Raisins (optional)
	Vegetable cooking spray
	Melted butter or margarine

Combine ½ cup water and yeast in a small bowl; let stand 5 minutes. Combine oats, brown sugar, oil, molasses and salt in a large bowl. Add 2 cups boiling water, stirring well. Stir in 2 cups cold water. Stir in yeast mixture. Stir in wheat germ, whole wheat flour and enough all-purpose flour to make a soft dough. Stir in nuts or raisins, if desired. Turn dough out onto a lightly floured surface and knead about 10 minutes until smooth and elastic. Divide dough in half and place in two well-greased bowls, turning to grease tops. Cover with a damp cloth and let rise in a warm place until doubled in bulk. Divide dough into four parts; knead and shape into loaves. Place in two, 8 ½ x 4 ½ x 2 ½-inch and two, 9 x 5 x 3-inch loaf pans that have been sprayed with cooking spray. Let loaves rise until gently rounded on top. (If they rise too high, they will fall in the oven.) Bake at 375 degrees for 45 minutes. Brush loaves with melted butter; remove from pans, and let cool on wire racks.

Yield: 4 loaves

Bread Machine Focaccia

Dough:

3 cups bread flour	½ teaspoon salt
2 ¼ teaspoons active dry yeast	1 cup plus 2 tablespoons water
½ teaspoon sugar	1 tablespoon olive oil

Topping:

6 tablespoons extra virgin olive oil, divided	¼ cup fresh sage leaves, snipped into pieces
2 large yellow onions, thinly sliced	1 ½ teaspoons coarse salt (kosher or sea)
	Freshly ground pepper

Combine dough ingredients in bread machine according to manufacturer's instructions. (All ingredients must be at room temperature.) Set bread machine on dough/manual setting. Press clear/stop at the end of the program. To punch dough down, press start and let knead for 60 seconds. Press clear/stop again. Remove dough and let rest 5 minutes before hand shaping. Sprinkle hands with flour. Spread dough evenly with fingertips into a lightly oiled 13 x 9 x 1-inch baking pan. Cover with a clean kitchen cloth. Let rise 30 to 60 minutes or until doubled in height. Heat 4 tablespoons oil in a medium skillet over low heat; add onion and sauté until tender and transparent. Do not brown. Spread onion over unbaked Focaccia. Sprinkle with sage, salt and pepper to taste. Drizzle with remaining 2 tablespoons oil. Bake on bottom rack at 400 degrees for 30 to 35 minutes or until golden brown. Let cool in pan. Cut and serve at room temperature.

Yield: 1 loaf focaccia

Aluminum foil (heavy duty or regular piece folded in half) under a napkin in a serving basket will help breads and rolls stay warm.

One Hour Yeast Rolls

¼ cup warm water (105 to 115 degrees)	½ cup sugar
2 (¼-ounce) envelopes active dry yeast	1 teaspoon salt
1 ½ cups buttermilk	4 ½ cups all-purpose flour
⅓ cup vegetable oil	½ teaspoon baking soda
	Melted butter

Combine water and yeast in a small bowl; let stand 5 minutes. Combine buttermilk, oil, sugar and salt in a large mixing bowl. Stir in yeast mixture. Combine flour and baking soda; stir into buttermilk mixture, mixing well. Let dough stand 10 minutes. Roll dough out onto a lightly floured surface and cut with round biscuit cutter. Place on greased baking pan and brush with melted butter. Let stand 30 minutes. Bake at 400 degrees for 15 to 18 minutes.

Yield: 1 ½ to 2 dozen

 # Sour Cream Yeast Rolls

¼ cup warm water (105 to 115 degrees)	2 tablespoons sugar
1 (¼-ounce) package active dry yeast	¼ teaspoon baking soda
2 cups sour cream	5 ½ cups buttermilk baking mix, divided

Combine water and yeast in a small bowl; let stand 5 minutes. Combine sour cream, sugar and baking soda in a large bowl. Stir in 2 cups of baking mix and yeast mixture, mixing well. Stir in 3 cups baking mix. Turn dough out onto a surface dusted with remaining ½ cup baking mix. Knead to form a smooth ball. Shape dough into 1-inch balls (about the size of a walnut). Place balls close together in a greased 13 x 9 x 2-inch baking pan. Let rise until doubled in bulk. Bake at 375 degrees for 15 minutes or until done. Rolls can be made ahead and frozen. When ready to serve, thaw rolls and reheat at 200 degrees.

Yield: 6 dozen

BREADS & BRUNCH

 # Sweet Roll Dough

½ cup warm water
(105 to 115 degrees)
2 (¼-ounce) envelopes active
dry yeast
1½ cups milk, lukewarm
2 large eggs, lightly beaten

½ cup sugar
½ cup shortening
2 teaspoons salt
7-7½ cups sifted all-purpose flour,
divided

Combine water and yeast in a small bowl; let stand 5 minutes. Combine milk, eggs, sugar, shortening and salt in a large mixing bowl. Stir in yeast mixture. Stir half of the flour into milk mixture, mixing well. Add enough remaining flour to make a soft dough. Turn dough out onto a lightly floured surface and knead until smooth and elastic. Place dough in a well-greased bowl, turning to grease top. Cover with a damp cloth and let rise in a warm place until doubled in bulk. Punch dough down; cover and refrigerate until ready to use. Divide dough in half. Use one half to make Dinner Rolls and the other half to make Butterscotch Rolls.

Butterscotch Rolls

⅓ cup butter, melted
½ cup firmly packed light brown
sugar
1 tablespoon corn syrup

½ Sweet Roll Dough
(see recipe above)
2 tablespoons butter, softened
½ cup sugar
2 teaspoons ground cinnamon

Combine melted butter, brown sugar and corn syrup in the bottom of a 13 x 9 x 2-inch baking pan; set aside. Roll dough into a 15 x 9-inch rectangle on a lightly floured surface. Spread with 2 tablespoons butter and sprinkle with sugar and cinnamon. Roll up tightly, beginning at wide edge. Pinch long edge of roll (do not seal ends). Cut roll into 1-inch slices. Place slices cut side down, in prepared pan. Let rise until doubled in size. Bake at 375 degrees for 25 to 30 minutes. Turn pan upside down immediately on a serving tray. Let pan stay over rolls about a minute so butterscotch syrup coats rolls.

Dinner Rolls

½ **Sweet Roll Dough**
   (See *Sweet Roll Dough* recipe on page 50.)

Shape dough into 2-inch balls; place on a lightly greased pan. Let rise until doubled in size. Bake at 400 degrees for 12 to 15 minutes.

 Angel Biscuits ✓

The dough will keep for several weeks in the refrigerator. It's handy to have on hand for company.

½ **cup warm water**	1 **teaspoon baking soda**
(105 to 115 degrees)	1 **teaspoon salt**
1 **(¼-ounce) envelope active dry**	½ **cup vegetable shortening**
yeast	2 **cups low-fat buttermilk**
5 **cups all-purpose flour**	**Vegetable cooking spray**
¼ **cup sugar**	1 **tablespoon butter or**
1 **teaspoon baking powder**	**margarine, melted**

Combine water and yeast in a small bowl; let stand 5 minutes. Combine flour, sugar, baking powder, baking soda and salt in a large bowl. Cut in shortening with a pastry blender or fork until mixture resembles a coarse meal. Add yeast mixture and buttermilk, stirring just until moist. Cover and refrigerate 1 hour. Turn dough out onto a heavily floured surface; knead lightly 5 times. Roll dough to a ½-inch thickness; cut with a 3-inch round biscuit cutter. Place biscuits on a baking sheet coated with cooking spray; brush with melted butter. Bake at 450 degrees for 13 minutes or until golden.

Yield: 2 dozen

🍃 Cheesy Cranberry Bread

The scrumptious smell of fresh baked fruit and nut breads make it hard to wait, but they are even better if stored 24 hours before serving.

1 ½ cups fresh cranberries, halved	1 cup milk
1 ¼ cups sugar, divided	½ cup butter, melted and cooled
2 cups all-purpose flour	½ cup walnuts, coarsely chopped
2 teaspoons baking powder	2 teaspoons grated orange peel
½ teaspoon salt	1 ½ cups (6 ounces) finely shredded cheddar cheese
1 large egg, lightly beaten	

Combine cranberries and ½ cup sugar; set aside. Combine flour, ¾ cup sugar, baking powder and salt in a large bowl; set aside. Combine milk, egg and butter; stir in walnuts, peel, and cheese. Add milk mixture to flour mixture, stirring only until moistened. Fold in cranberries. Spoon mixture into a lightly greased 9 x 5 x 3-inch loaf pan. Bake at 350 degrees for 60 minutes. Cool in pan 10 minutes; remove from pan, and let cool on wire rack.

Yield: 1 loaf

🍃 Vidalia Onion Supper Bread

2 tablespoons butter or margarine	½ cup sour cream
½ cup chopped Vidalia onion	½ cup shredded sharp cheddar cheese
1 (8 ½-ounce) package corn muffin mix	

Heat butter in a small skillet over medium-high heat; add onion and sauté until tender, but not brown. Prepare muffin mix according to package directions. Spoon into a greased 8 x 8x 2-inch baking pan. Sprinkle with onion. Combine sour cream and cheese; spoon over top of batter. Bake at 400 degrees for 15 minutes or until done.

Aunt Nellie's Date and Nut Bread

1	(8-ounce) box chopped dates	¾	cup firmly packed light brown sugar
1	tablespoon shortening		
1	cup boiling water	1	teaspoon baking soda
1	large egg, lightly beaten	½	teaspoon salt
2	cups all-purpose flour	½	teaspoon ground cinnamon
		½	cup chopped nuts

Combine dates, shortening and boiling water in a large bowl; cool. Stir in egg, flour, brown sugar, soda, salt and cinnamon, mixing until just blended. Fold in nuts. Spoon mixture into a greased 9 x 5 x 3-inch loaf pan or two, 8 x 4 x 2½-inch loaf pans. Bake at 300 degrees for 45 minutes or until a toothpick inserted in the center comes out clean. Cool in pan(s) for 3 minutes, then cool on wire rack. Flavor is enhanced if baked one day in advance. Slice and serve with cream cheese.

Carrot Tea Bread

3	large eggs	1½ teaspoons ground cinnamon
1½ cups sugar		1 teaspoon baking soda
¾	cup vegetable oil	¼ teaspoon salt
2¾ cups all-purpose flour		1½ cups finely shredded carrots
1¾ teaspoons baking powder		Powdered sugar (optional)

Grease a 9 x 5 x 3-inch loaf pan. Line bottom of pan with wax paper; grease. Beat eggs, sugar and oil in a large mixing bowl with a rotary beater or whisk until well blended. Combine flour, baking powder, cinnamon, soda and salt; stir into egg mixture. Stir in carrots. Spoon batter into prepared pan. Bake at 325 degrees for 1 hour 20 minutes or until a toothpick inserted in the center comes out clean. Cool in pan 10 minutes; remove from pan, peel off wax paper and let cool on wire rack. Sprinkle with powdered sugar, if desired.

Yield: 1 loaf

Very Best Cornbread

1 (8-ounce) container sour cream	1 (12-ounce) package
3 large eggs, lightly beaten	cornbread mix
½ cup vegetable oil	1 (8 ½-ounce) can cream-style
½ teaspoon salt	corn

Combine sour cream, eggs, ½ cup oil and salt in a large bowl. Stir in cornbread mix and corn. Place a well-greased 8-inch cast-iron skillet in a 400 degree oven for 3 to 5 minutes or until hot. Remove from oven; spoon batter into skillet. Bake at 400 degrees for 30 to 40 minutes or until lightly browned.

Yield: 6 servings

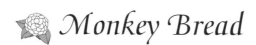 Monkey Bread

½ cup sugar	1 tablespoon ground cinnamon
½ cup firmly packed light brown sugar	3 (12-ounce) cans refrigerated buttermilk biscuits
¼ cup finely chopped nuts	½ cup butter, melted

Combine sugar, brown sugar, nuts and cinnamon in a small bowl. Open 1 can of biscuits and cut each into quarters. Roll pieces into balls and roll in sugar mixture. (You may also toss biscuit balls, a few at a time, with the sugar in a plastic bag.) Place balls in the bottom of a greased Bundt pan. Drizzle with ⅓ of melted butter. Repeat twice with remaining ingredients. Sprinkle the top with remaining sugar mixture. Bake at 350 degrees for 30 to 35 minutes. Cool 5 minutes; turn out onto a serving plate. Serve warm.

Herb and Cheese Pull Aparts

1	(8-ounce) package cream cheese, softened
1	teaspoon dried parsley
1	teaspoon dried basil
1	teaspoon chopped chives
½	teaspoon dill seed
⅛	teaspoon garlic powder
1	(8-ounce) package refrigerated crescent rolls
1	large egg, lightly beaten
½	teaspoon poppy seeds

Combine cream cheese, parsley, basil, chives, dill seed and garlic powder in a small bowl; set aside. Unroll crescent rolls into 2 rectangles; press edges together to make 1 long rectangle. Press perforations to seal. Spread cheese mixture over dough to within ½-inch of edge. Roll, starting with the long side, jelly-roll fashion. Pinch edges to seal. Place on a lightly greased baking sheet. Cut ½-inch slices, using kitchen shears, alternating from right to left side of dough. Do not cut completely through the dough. Pull out alternating sides of roll, exposing spiral pattern. Brush with eggs and sprinkle with poppy seeds. Bake at 375 degrees for 12 to 15 minutes.

Yield: 6 to 8 servings

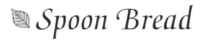 Spoon Bread

2	cups milk	½	teaspoon salt
½	cup white cornmeal	3	large eggs, lightly beaten
3	tablespoons butter		

Pour milk into a 2-quart saucepan over medium heat. Slowly stir in cornmeal. Cook, stirring occasionally, until mixture is thickened. Remove from heat; stir in butter and salt, mixing well. Let cool 15 minutes. Fold eggs into cooled mixture. Pour into a greased 1½-quart baking dish. Bake at 350 degrees for 45 to 55 minutes or until nicely puffed and top is lightly browned. Serve immediately with butter.

Yield: 4 servings

BREADS & BRUNCH

 # Skillet Buttermilk Biscuits

2	cups all-purpose flour	⅛	teaspoon salt
4	teaspoons baking powder	½	cup butter, divided
¼	teaspoon baking soda	¾-1	cup buttermilk

Combine flour, baking powder, baking soda and salt in a large bowl. Cut in 4 tablespoons butter with a pastry blender or fork until mixture resembles a coarse meal. Add buttermilk, stirring just until dry ingredients are moistened. Turn dough out onto a lightly floured surface. Roll dough to a ½-inch thickness; cut with a 2½-inch round biscuit cutter. Place 2 tablespoons butter in a 10½-inch cast-iron skillet and place in a 350 degree oven for 5 minutes until butter melts. Remove from oven and place biscuits in skillet. Bake at 350 degrees for 20 minutes or until golden. Melt remaining butter and brush over tops of rolls.

Yield: 1 dozen

Cheese N' Dill Scones

2½	cups all-purpose flour	1⅓	cups (5 ounces) shredded cheddar cheese, divided
¼	cup fresh parsley, chopped		
1	tablespoon baking powder	½	cup light or nonfat sour cream
2	teaspoons dried dill weed		
½	teaspoon salt	2	large eggs, lightly beaten
¾	cup butter	¼	cup milk

Combine flour, parsley, baking powder, dill and salt in a large bowl. Cut in butter with a pastry blender or fork until mixture resembles a coarse meal. Stir in 1 cup cheese. Add sour cream, eggs and milk eggs, stirring just until moistened. Turn dough out onto a lightly floured surface; knead 1 minute. Divide dough in half; roll each half into an 8-inch circle. Cut each circle into 8 wedges and place 1-inch apart on a baking sheet. Sprinkle each evenly with remaining cheese. Bake at 400 degrees for 13 minutes or until lightly browned.

Yield: 16 servings

BREADS & BRUNCH

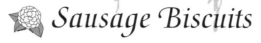 # Sausage Biscuits

1 (8-ounce) package extra sharp cheese, shredded	1 (1-pound) package hot sausage
	2 cups buttermilk baking mix

Combine cheese, sausage and baking mix in a large bowl until well blended. Drop and shape into bite-size biscuits on an ungreased baking sheet. Bake at 400 degrees for 15 to 20 minutes until lightly browned. Recipe may be frozen. Reheat in the oven for about 18 minutes.

Yield: about 4 dozen

Almond Puff

1 cup plus 2 tablespoons butter or margarine, divided	2 ½ teaspoons almond extract, divided
2 cups all-purpose flour, divided	3 large eggs
1 ¼ cups water, divided	1 ½ cups sifted powdered sugar

Cut ½ cup butter into 1 cup flour with a pastry blender or fork until mixture resembles a coarse meal. Add 2 tablespoons water; stir with a fork until ingredients are moistened. Shape into a ball and divide in half. Shape each half into a 12 x 3-inch rectangle on an ungreased baking sheet. Rectangles should be about 3 inches apart. Combine 1 cup water and ½ cup butter in a medium saucepan over medium heat; bring to a rolling boil. Remove from heat; quickly stir in 1 teaspoon almond extract and 1 cup flour. Stir over heat about 1 minute until mixture forms a ball. Remove from heat. Beat in eggs until smooth; spread mixture over pastry rectangles, covering completely. Bake at 350 degrees for 45 to 60 minutes. Cool completely. Combine powdered sugar, 2 tablespoons butter, 1 ½ teaspoons almond extract and 1 to 2 tablespoons warm water, stirring until smooth. Spread evenly over puffs.

BREADS & BRUNCH

 # Lemon-Poppyseed Muffins

1	(18 ½-ounce) package yellow cake mix with pudding	4	large eggs, lightly beaten
⅔	cup vegetable oil	⅓	cup poppyseeds
⅔	cup apricot nectar	½	teaspoon grated lemon peel
		2 ½	tablespoons fresh lemon juice

Combine cake mix, oil, nectar, eggs, poppyseeds, lemon peel and juice in a large bowl. Spoon into greased muffin pans, filling two-thirds full. Bake at 400 degrees for 18 to 20 minutes or until golden brown.

Yield: about 2 dozen

 # Oven-Baked French Toast

¼	cup butter, melted	½	cup orange juice
2	tablespoons honey		Pinch salt
½	teaspoon ground cinnamon	6	slices whole wheat bread
3	large eggs, lightly beaten		

Combine butter, honey and cinnamon in a small bowl, stirring well. Pour into a 13 x 9 x 2-inch baking pan. Combine eggs, orange juice and salt in a shallow bowl. Dip bread slices into egg mixture, coating well. Drain and arrange on top of honey mixture. Bake at 400 degrees for 20 minutes or until browned. Turn over onto serving plate. Serve with Honey Butter.

Yield: 6 servings

Honey Butter:

3	tablespoons butter, softened	¼	cup honey

Combine butter and honey. Serve at room temperature.

Yield: ⅓ cup

BREADS & BRUNCH

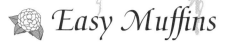
Easy Muffins

1 **cup self-rising flour**	¼ **cup mayonnaise**
½ **cup milk**	

Combine ingredients in a bowl. Spoon batter into a lightly greased muffin pan. Bake at 350 degrees for 20 minutes.

Old Attic Recipes—This cook has always been attracted to "attic recipes"; those old recipes found on dog-eared and yellowing bits of paper stored in an old cupboard or up in grandmother's attic.

Fat-Free Bran Muffins

1 **cup oat bran (oat bran hot cereal)**	1 ¼ **cups whole wheat flour**
1 **cup skim milk**	2 **teaspoons baking powder**
1 **large egg, lightly beaten**	1 **cup fresh or frozen blueberries (optional)**
¼ **cup sugar or sugar substitute equal to ¼ cup sugar**	

Combine bran and milk in a large bowl; stir in egg and sugar. Combine flour and baking powder. Add to egg mixture, stirring just until ingredients are moistened. Fold in blueberries, if desired. Spoon batter into a greased muffin pan. Bake at 400 degrees for 20 to 25 minutes. Muffins may be frozen when cool.

Yield: 1 dozen

 Whole Wheat Pancakes

1 ½-2 cups milk	½ cup unbleached all-purpose
⅓ cup vegetable oil	flour
2 large eggs	3 tablespoons brown sugar
1 ½ cups whole wheat flour	4 teaspoons baking powder
	¾ teaspoon salt

Combine milk, oil, eggs, flours, sugar, baking powder and salt in a blender. Process for 10 seconds. Scrape down sides of container and process for 10 more seconds. Pour about ¼-cup batter onto a hot, greased griddle. Turn pancakes when tops are covered with bubbles. Serve with honey, if desired.

Yield: 16 (4-inch) pancakes

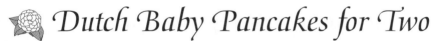 Dutch Baby Pancakes for Two

This pancake rises in all directions, it is really interesting.

½ cup all-purpose flour	½ cup skim milk
1 tablespoon sugar	1 tablespoon butter, melted
2 large eggs, lightly beaten	1 teaspoon vanilla extract

Combine flour and sugar; set aside. Combine eggs, milk, butter and vanilla in a small bowl. Add to dry ingredients, stirring well. Pour into a well greased 8 x 8-inch or 9 x 9-inch baking pan. Bake at 450 degrees for 20 minutes, turn off oven and bake for 2 more minutes until puffed and golden. Cut in half and serve with syrup.

BREADS & BRUNCH

True German Apple Pancakes

½ cup milk	2 tablespoons butter
½ cup all-purpose flour	1 tablespoon cinnamon
3 eggs	1 tablespoon powdered sugar
1 teaspoon sugar	1 tablespoon butter
1 large apple, peeled and sliced	

Melt 2 tablespoons of butter in a 10-inch ovenproof skillet. Sauté apple slices in skillet until softened. Beat together milk, eggs, flour and sugar until well blended. Pour batter over the apples. Bake in a 500 degree oven for 10 minutes. Sift cinnamon and powdered sugar over top and dot with butter. Bake until brown (3 to 4 minutes). Serve hot.

Yield: 2 to 3 servings

Breakfast Pie

1 (9-inch) unbaked pie shell	1 tablespoon green pepper, chopped
1 ½ cups (6 ounces) shredded mozzarella	4 large eggs
4 ounces cooked turkey sausage	¾ cup milk
¼ cup mushrooms, chopped	Salt
1 tablespoon onion, chopped	Pepper

Prick bottom of pie shell with a fork. Bake at 400 degrees for 8 minutes; cool. Place half of cheese in the bottom of cooled pie shell. Top with sausage, mushrooms, onion and green pepper. Sprinkle with remaining cheese. Whisk together eggs, milk, salt and pepper in a small bowl until well blended. Pour into shell. Bake at 350 degrees for 45 minutes or until knife inserted in center comes out clean.

Yield: 4 to 6 servings

BREADS & BRUNCH

French Toast

8	(1-inch thick) slices French bread	⅛	teaspoon salt
4	large eggs	2	tablespoons butter or margarine, divided
1	cup milk		Powdered sugar
2	tablespoons orange juice		Orange Sauce
½	teaspoon vanilla extract		

Place bread in a 13 x 9 x 2-inch baking dish. Beat together eggs, milk, juice, vanilla and salt. Pour mixture over bread slices; turn slices to evenly coat. Cover and refrigerate overnight. Heat 1 tablespoon butter in a large skillet. Sauté 4 slices of soaked bread for 5 minutes on each side or until lightly browned. Repeat with remaining butter and bread slices. Sprinkle toast with powdered sugar; serve immediately with Orange Sauce.

Yield: 8 servings

Orange Sauce:

1	cup firmly packed light brown sugar	2	teaspoons grated orange peel (optional)
		½	cup orange juice

Combine sugar, peel and juice in a small saucepan, stirring well. Bring mixture to a boil; reduce heat and simmer, stirring frequently, until mixture is thickened.

Yield: 1 ¼ cups

Self-rising flour = 4 cups flour, 2 teaspoons salt and 2 tablespoons baking powder. Mix well and store in a tightly covered container.

BREADS & BRUNCH

French Toast Fingers

2	large eggs	½	cup strawberry preserves
¼	cup milk	8	slices day old bread
¼	teaspoon salt		Powdered sugar (optional)

Beat eggs, milk and salt in a small bowl. Spread preserves on 4 slices of bread; top with remaining 4 slices. Trim crusts and cut each into three strips. Dip strips in egg mixture, coating well. Cook strips on a hot, lightly greased griddle for 2 minutes on each side or until golden brown. Sprinkle with powdered sugar, if desired.

Yield: 4 servings

Bacon and Egg Strata

9	tablespoons butter, divided	12	large or jumbo eggs, lightly beaten
¾	cup dry bread crumbs		Salt
12	slices crisp, cooked bacon, drained and crumbled		Pepper
2¾	cups milk	1	(8-ounce) package sliced Swiss cheese
3	cups soft, fresh bread crumbs		

Heat 3 tablespoons butter in a small skillet. Stir in dry bread crumbs and bacon; set aside. Combine milk and soft bread crumbs in a bowl until bread crumbs are thoroughly soaked through. Drain bread crumbs, reserving milk. Combine milk with eggs, salt and pepper. Heat 6 tablespoons butter in a large skillet; pour in egg mixture; cook until soft and not fully cooked. Add the soft bread crumbs; stir gently. Spoon the partially cooked egg mixture into a greased 13 x 9 x 2-inch baking dish. Place Swiss cheese slices over the top. Sprinkle with bacon-bread crumb mixture. Cover and refrigerate 8 hours or overnight. Remove 1 hour before baking. Bake, uncovered, at 425 degrees for 20 to 25 minutes or until cooked and hot in the center. Cut into squares. Serve with coffee cake and skewered fruit.

Yield: 12 to 14 servings

Creamy Eggplant Tomato Pie

*A luscious vegetable pie that can be made with
all garden vegetables. Serve with a salad and crusty bread.*

4 tablespoons butter, divided	1 tablespoon lemon juice
3 tablespoons diced onion	2 tablespoons fresh minced
2 cloves garlic, minced	basil or ¾ teaspoon dried
1 cup diced red bell pepper	Salt
1 cup diced green bell pepper	Pepper
5 cups diced, peeled eggplant	1 (10-inch) unbaked pie shell
¼ cup water	2 large tomatoes, sliced
1 (8-ounce) package cream	½ cup wheat germ
cheese, cubed	¼ cup bread crumbs
5 tablespoons grated Parmesan	
cheese, divided	

Heat 2 tablespoons butter in a large skillet; sauté onion, garlic and peppers for 5 minutes or until tender. Add eggplant and water. Cover and cook for 5 minutes, stirring occasionally. Add cream cheese; cook, stirring occasionally until cheese melts. Stir in 2 tablespoons Parmesan cheese, lemon juice and basil. Season to taste with salt and pepper. Spoon half of eggplant mixture into pie shell. Cover with tomato slices and top with remaining eggplant mixture. Melt remaining 2 tablespoons butter in a small skillet; stir in wheat germ, bread crumbs and remaining 3 tablespoon of Parmesan cheese. Sprinkle topping over pie. Bake at 350 degrees for 40 minutes. Serve hot.

Yield: 8 servings

When milk is used in making bread, you get a finer texture. Water makes coarser bread.

BREADS & BRUNCH

Brunch Sausage Strata

10 slices white bread	2 tablespoons butter or
2 (8-ounce) packages Monterey	vegetable oil
Jack cheese, shredded	1 (8-ounce) package
1-2 pounds bulk pork sausage	mushrooms, sliced
5 large eggs	1 (10 ¾-ounce) can cream of
2 ¼ cups milk	mushroom soup
¾ teaspoon dry mustard	

Trim crusts from bread and cut into cubes. Spread in a lightly greased 13 x 9 x 2-inch baking dish. Sprinkle with cheese. Brown sausage in a large skillet, stirring until it crumbles; drain. Spread over cheese. Beat eggs, milk and dry mustard together in a small bowl; pour over cheese. Cover and refrigerate 8 hours or overnight. Heat butter in a large skillet over medium-high heat; sauté mushrooms until tender. (You may substitute drained, canned mushrooms.) Spread mushrooms over strata; spread soup over mushrooms. Bake at 325 degrees for 1 ½ hours or until center is set.

Yield: 8 to 10 servings

Potato-Salsa Frittata

Frittatas are to Italians what omelets are to the French. They are easier to prepare for a crowd than omelets. A perfect dish for a brunch.

2	teaspoons olive oil	¼	teaspoon coarse ground pepper
3-4	red potatoes, cubed		
6	large eggs	¼	cup shredded sharp cheddar cheese
1	(11 to 12-ounce) jar of medium-hot salsa, divided		
		1	tomato, chopped
½	teaspoon salt		Salsa

Heat olive oil in a 10-inch ovenproof nonstick skillet over medium-high heat. Add potatoes and cook, covered, for 10 minutes, stirring occasionally, or until potatoes are tender and golden brown. Whisk together eggs, ¼ cup salsa, salt and pepper; stir in cheese. Stir egg mixture into potatoes and cook over medium heat, covered, for 3 minutes or until egg mixture begins to set around edge. Remove cover and place skillet in a 425 degree oven. Bake 4 to 6 minutes or until frittata is set. Transfer frittata to a cutting board. Cut into wedges and top with salsa and tomato.

Yield: 4 main dish servings

Old Amish Proverb: Eat it up, wear it out, make it do, or do without!

BREADS & BRUNCH

Christmas Morning Sausage-Egg Dish

½ pound bulk sausage, cooked and drained	½ cup plus 2 tablespoons buttermilk baking mix
2 ounces fresh mushrooms, sliced	6 large eggs, lightly beaten
¼ cup sliced green onions	½ cup milk
1 tomato, chopped	¼ teaspoon salt
1 cup (4 ounces) shredded Mozzarella cheese	¼ teaspoon dried oregano
	Dash pepper

Layer sausage, mushroom, green onion, tomato and cheese in a greased 8 x 8-inch baking dish. Cover and refrigerate until ready to cook. Combine baking mix, eggs, milk, salt, oregano and pepper in a bowl. Pour over sausage mixture. Bake at 350 degrees for 50 minutes or until golden brown and set. Cut into squares and serve.

Yield: 4 servings

 # Mock Fried Apples

Goes well with sausage for a delicious breakfast.

1 cooking apple (per person), peeled and sliced	Light brown sugar
Ground cinnamon or nutmeg	Butter

Layer apple slices in a buttered baking dish; sprinkle with cinnamon or nutmeg and brown sugar. Dot with butter. Bake at 350 degrees for 1 hour.

Sausage-Cheese Bake

1	pound bulk pork sausage	2	tablespoons chopped green pepper
1	(8-ounce) can refrigerated crescent rolls	4	large eggs, lightly beaten
2	(8-ounce) packages Monterey Jack cheese, shredded	¾	cup milk
		½	teaspoon dried oregano
		⅛	teaspoon pepper

Brown sausage in a large skillet, stirring until it crumbles; drain. Unroll crescent rolls into 2 rectangles. Place dough on the bottom and ½-inch up the sides of a lightly greased 13 x 9 x 2-inch baking dish, press perforations to seal. Sprinkle sausage over dough; top with cheese and pepper. Combine eggs, milk, oregano and pepper; pour over casserole. Bake at 400 degrees for 18 to 20 minutes.

Yield: 8 servings

 # Tuna Casserole

*We find many tuna casseroles are boring fare. Not this one—
the different ingredients spark it up. Try it for a brunch. Teenagers
like to make this because it is made in one dish.*

2	(6 ½-ounce) cans water packed tuna, drained	½	cup sliced ripe olives
1	cup sour cream	½	cup cashews
¾	cup canned sliced mushrooms, drained or ¾ cup sliced fresh mushrooms, sautéed	¼	teaspoon dried oregano
			Shredded cheddar cheese

Combine tuna, sour cream, mushrooms, olives, cashews and oregano in a bowl. Spoon into a lightly greased 1 ½-quart baking dish. Sprinkle with cheese. Bake at 350 degrees for 25 to 30 minutes or until hot and bubbly.

BREADS & BRUNCH

Sweet Vidalia Onion Pie

*This is an easy recipe that, with a green salad,
makes a nice lunch or light dinner. Adding ½ cup cooked
green vegetables will add color to this dish.*

1 ½ cups fine cracker crumbs (about 40 saltines or buttery round crackers)	3 large eggs, lightly beaten
⅓ cup butter, melted	1 cup milk
3 tablespoons butter	1 teaspoon salt
3 cups thinly sliced Vidalia or other sweet onion (about 3 large)	¼ teaspoon pepper
	1 (8-ounce) package cheddar cheese, finely shredded

Combine cracker crumbs and melted butter in a bowl; press firmly and evenly into a 9-inch pie plate. Heat 3 tablespoons butter in a large skillet over medium-high heat; add onions and sauté until golden brown. Spoon onions into crust. Combine eggs, milk, salt and pepper; stir in cheese. Pour cheese mixture over onions. Bake at 350 degrees for 30 to 40 minutes or until knife inserted 1 inch from edge comes out clean.

Yield: 6 to 8 servings

 When cooking in glass pans reduce oven temperature by 25 degrees.

Cookin' Low Country

The livin's easy with savory Low Country dishes. This section of *Twice Treasured Recipes* is filled with mouth-watering old-fashioned and modern Southern *receipts*. Recipes in the Low Country are often referred to as *receipts* and as late as the 1930's no less an authority than the Oxford Dictionary of Good Usage listed *"Receipt-Recipe-In the sense of a formula for the making of a food or a medicine, either word is as good as the other."* In other words, a receipt is a recipe by another name.

The photo for *Cookin' Low Country* is a renowned Low Country scene of a trolling shrimp boat in the Atlantic Ocean near the beaches of Sea Pines Plantation, with Sea Oats rippling in the foreground on an early fall afternoon breeze.

Cookin' Low Country includes traditional favorites like *Melt in Your Mouth Corn Bread* and *Really Red Rice,* which are always delicious with fresh shrimp, no matter how you cook it; or *Hilton Head Hush Puppies* served with fragrant, rich, creamy *She-Crab Soup.*

Our collection of *Twice Treasured Recipes* would not be complete without a variety of appetizing methods for preparing Low Country seafood sure to please the most discriminating palates; and don't overlook our playful *Hilton Head Fruitcake* receipt, leavened with a heapin' handful of humor. Amble on into the kitchen and start *Cookin' Low Country.*

Cookin'
Low Country

Cookin' Low Country

Quick and Easy Recipes are designated with a camellia flower.

Memorable Menu Recipes are designated with a leaf.

 Really Red Rice ✓

*This traditional southern dish is easy to prepare and very flavorful.
It's delicious when served with ham, seafood, steak or pork.*

4	slices bacon	1	cup bouillon
1	small sweet onion, chopped	¾	cup tomato juice
2	cups uncooked rice	½	teaspoon salt
1	(14 ½-ounce) can diced tomatoes	¼	teaspoon pepper
		⅛	teaspoon pepper sauce

Fry bacon in a large skillet over medium-high heat until crisp; remove from pan and drain on paper towels. Crumble and set aside. Heat pan with bacon drippings over medium-high heat. Add onion and sauté until soft, but not brown. Spoon onion into a lightly greased baking dish. Sauté rice in bacon drippings over low heat until rice is light brown. Spoon rice over onion; add diced tomatoes, bouillon, tomato juice, salt, pepper and pepper sauce. For a spicier dish, add more hot sauce. Top with crumbled bacon and cover tightly. Bake at 350 degrees for 1 hour.

Yield: 6 servings

Hilton Head Hush Puppies

2	cups cornmeal	½	cup water
2	teaspoons baking powder	1	sweet onion, chopped
1	teaspoon salt		Vegetable oil or shortening
1	teaspoon sugar		for frying
1 ½	cups milk		

Combine cornmeal, baking powder, salt and sugar; stir until well blended. Combine milk and water and stir into dry ingredients. Stir in onion (dough will be stiff). Roll dough into bite size balls and fry in deep fat until well browned. Drain on paper towels. Place in a warm oven to keep warm until ready to serve.

Bluffton She-Crab Soup

2	cups milk		Pepper
¼	teaspoon mace		Cayenne pepper
2	cups flaked crabmeat	½	cup crushed saltine crackers
	(fresh or frozen)	2	tablespoons sherry
2	cups light cream		Chopped fresh parsley
3	tablespoons butter		(optional)
	Salt		

Combine milk and mace in top of a double boiler; bring water to a boil. Reduce heat to low; cook 8 minutes. Stir in crabmeat, cream and butter. Season to taste with salt, pepper and cayenne. Cook 15 minutes, stirring occasionally, over low heat. Remove from heat. Stir in crushed crackers and let stand several minutes to thicken soup. Stir in sherry just before serving. Sprinkle each serving with parsley, if desired.

Yield: 6 servings

Bar-B-Q Pig's Feet

6-8 split pig's feet
1 large onion, chopped
5 cloves garlic, minced
2 stalks celery, chopped

6-8 fresh sage leaves
2 bay leaves
1 teaspoon salt

Sauce:
1 cup barbecue sauce
1 cup cane syrup
1 cup ketchup
2 tablespoons prepared
   mustard

1 tablespoon vanilla extract
1 teaspoon nutmeg
1 teaspoon ground cinnamon

Combine pig's feet, onion, garlic, celery, sage, bay leaves and salt in a large skillet over medium heat. Cook pig's feet in boiling water for 1 ½ to 2 hours until tender; transfer to a large baking pan. Combine barbecue sauce, cane syrup, ketchup, mustard, vanilla, nutmeg and cinnamon in a large bowl; mix well. Pour sauce over the meat. Bake at 350 degrees for 50 minutes to 1 hour.

Yield: 6 to 8 servings

 # Penn Center Oyster Stew

¼ cup butter or margarine
1 pint fresh oysters
2 cups milk
½ cup light cream

1 teaspoon salt
   Dash pepper
   Dash paprika

Melt butter in a small saucepan over low heat. Add oysters; cook, stirring constantly, just until edges curl. Combine milk and cream in a medium saucepan over medium heat. Add oyster mixture and salt. Season with pepper; sprinkle with paprika.

Yield: 4 (1-cup) servings

76

COOKIN' LOW COUNTRY

Penn Center Conch Stew

5	conchs	1	tablespoon black pepper
3	pieces Joe Louis strips (ribs)	1	tablespoon garlic powder
	or smoked neck bone	1 ½	cups water
1	large onion, chopped		

Clean and dice conch. Place conch, strips, onion, pepper and garlic powder in a pressure cooker. Pour water over all ingredients. Cook according to manufacturer's directions for 35 minutes. Allow pressure to subside before opening. Check for tenderness of meat, if not ready, cook for 15 additional minutes. If you do not have a pressure cooker, cook in a tightly covered pan for 1 hour. Serve over rice.

Yield: about 6 servings

The Bargain Box has been an ardent supporter of our Program for Academic and Cultural Enrichment (PACE) here at Penn Center. Largely because of your support, we have realized our vision of a youth program positively impacting the academic and social development of thousands of children and their families. PACE students are scoring higher on standardized tests, achieving higher grade point averages, high school dropout is almost nonexistent among them and, with few exceptions, they continue on with post-high school education. Nearly 2000 students have experienced PACE during the past 16 years. As the students move from adolescence to adulthood, we believe we can help them learn the importance of their role in the prosperity of the entire community.

The Bargain Box truly practices the old African adage, "It takes an entire village to raise a child," through your many years of support.

Emory S. Campbell
Executive Director

Governor John C. West's Shrimp Stew

I first had this shrimp stew on Kiawah Island when six of us owned a home there. It was long before the development of the Island, and the stew was made by an elderly black man. After watching him, I started making the dish and later served it regularly at legislative breakfasts at the Governor's mansion from 1971 to 1975. It's still a favorite brunch dish that we serve with homemade biscuits (my other specialty!).

5 slices (streak of lean) bacon	1 ½ teaspoons Worcestershire
3 medium onions, chopped	sauce
3 tablespoons all-purpose flour	Salt
2 cups water	Pepper
½ cup milk	2 cups small (creek) shrimp
2 tablespoons white wine	

Fry bacon in a large skillet over medium heat. Add chopped onions to drippings and sauté until tender. Stir in flour; cook 1 minute, stirring constantly. Stir in water, milk, wine and Worcestershire. Season to taste with salt and pepper. Cook, stirring frequently, until mixture is thickened. Stir in shrimp; cook until thoroughly heated, adding more water if necessary. Serve over hot grits.

Yield: about 10 servings

*The most indispensable ingredient
of all good cooking—love
for those you are cooking for.*

Crowne Plaza Resort's Calibogue Red Seafood Stew

1   cup olive oil
¼   cup minced garlic
1   cup yellow onion, diced ½-inch
2   cups yellow, red and green bell peppers, diced ¾-inch
1   pound peeled and deveined shrimp
½   pound scallops
½   pound peeled crawfish tails
½   pint shucked clams, or canned
½   pound boneless, skinless fish pieces
½   gallon marinara sauce
1   quart diced tomatoes, undrained
1   quart Port wine
½   gallon fish stock or clam juice
½   cup sugar
1   tablespoon Old Bay seasoning

1   tablespoon Cajun blackening spice
1   tablespoon Jamaican jerk dry seasoning
1   tablespoon dried oregano
1   teaspoon black pepper
1   teaspoon crushed fennel seeds
1   teaspoon ground cloves
4   bay leaves
¼   cup Worcestershire sauce
¼   cup green pepper sauce
1   pint shucked oysters and liquor
½   cup lemon juice
1   pound claw or lump crabmeat
2   handfuls fresh basil leaves, finely shredded
1   handful fresh spinach, finely shredded

Heat oil in a large soup pot over medium heat. Add garlic and sauté 1 to 2 minutes. Add onion and bell peppers; sauté, stirring constantly, until tender. Stir in shrimp, scallops, crawfish, clams and fish, tossing gently until they begin to cook. Add marinara, tomatoes and Port; stirring well. Add fish stock, sugar, Old Bay, Cajun seasoning, jerk seasoning, oregano, pepper, fennel, cloves and bay leaves; stirring until well blended. Stir in Worcestershire and green pepper sauce. Bring mixture to a boil, reduce heat and simmer for 5 minutes. Stir in oysters and lemon juice. Stir in crab, basil and spinach. If desired, keep adding your choice of seafood and liquid as needed (it just gets better).

Yield: 2¾ gallons or 30 servings

Chef Roosevelt Brownlee, Jr.'s Shrimp Gumbo

2 ½ quarts water, divided
1 pound peeled and deveined shrimp
1 teaspoon salt
¼ cup vegetable oil
1 cup diced onions
1 cup diced celery
1 cup diced bell pepper
½ teaspoon dried thyme
¼ teaspoon dried sage
¼ teaspoon rosemary
1 bay leaf
1 (4-ounce) can tomato paste
1 (20-ounce) can tomatoes (or 6 chopped fresh)
1 pound cut okra (fresh, canned or frozen)
1 cup green lima beans
1 cup cut corn
1 teaspoon black pepper

Heat 2 cups water and 1 teaspoon salt in a large saucepan over high heat until boiling. Add shrimp and cook 3 minutes. Drain, reserving liquid. Heat oil in a large soup pot over medium-high heat. Add onion, celery and bell pepper; sauté until tender. Stir in thyme, sage, rosemary and bay leaf. Stir in tomato paste; sauté for 1 minute. Stir in tomatoes, okra, lima beans, corn, pepper and remaining 2 quarts of water. Bring mixture to a boil, reduce heat to medium, and simmer for 20 minutes. When okra is tender, stir in cooked shrimp and as much reserved shrimp stock as needed.

Yield: 15 to 18 cups

Hyatt Regency Hilton Head
She-Crab Soup

1	stalk celery
½	carrot, peeled
¼	medium onion
10	tablespoons butter
1	cup all-purpose flour
4	(14-ounce) cans clam broth
2	crab bouillon cubes
½	teaspoon Old Bay seasoning
1	bay leaf

Pinch dried thyme
Pinch crushed red pepper
   flakes
Black pepper
1 pound ~~snow~~ crabmeat
1 cup sherry
   Dash hot pepper sauce
1 ½ cups heavy whipping cream

Place celery, carrot and onion in a food processor; process until very finely chopped. Melt butter in a soup pot over medium heat; add vegetables and sauté for 2 minutes. Add flour; cook, stirring constantly, for 1 minute. Add broth, bouillon, Old Bay, bay leaf, thyme and red pepper. Season to taste with pepper. Bring mixture to a boil, reduce heat to low, and simmer for 20 minutes. Add crabmeat, sherry and hot sauce; simmer 10 minutes. Stir in cream and serve.

Yield: 1 gallon

 *Carolina Iced Tea*

Tea is the world's most popular beverage except water and iced tea is South Carolina's state beverage. In 1799, South Carolina was the first place in the U.S. to grow tea and the only state to have produced tea commercially. The Low Country continues to commercially produce tea and it's found in area grocery stores and specialty shops. Here are four sure fire ways to prepare the Low Country's favorite beverage.

Microwave Tea

Place one quart of fresh, cold water in a microwave-safe container. Add 7 tea bags and heat on HIGH for 5 minutes. (Never use bags with metal staples.) Steep for an additional 5 minutes or to desired strength. Squeeze and remove tea bags. Add 3 quarts of fresh, cold water to make 1 gallon. Sweeten to taste; let cool. Pour over ice or refrigerate.

Brewed Tea

Use 7 tea bags for 1 gallon of iced tea. Bring 1 quart of fresh cold water to a rolling boil and pour over tea bags. Brew 5 minutes or to desired strength. Squeeze and remove tea bags. Add 3 quarts of fresh cold water. Sweeten to taste; let cool. Pour over ice or refrigerate.

Sun Tea

Place 7 tea bags in a gallon container filled with fresh cold water. Cap loosely and place in the sunshine away from combustible material for 3 to 4 hours. Squeeze and remove tea bags. Sweeten to taste. Pour over ice or refrigerate.

Moon Tea

Place 7 tea bags in a gallon container filled with fresh cold water. Cap loosely and let stand at room temperature for 6 hours or overnight. Squeeze and remove tea bags. Sweeten to taste. Pour over ice or refrigerate.

Hannah's Casserole

8 ¼ cups water, divided
1 ½ pounds unpeeled medium
    fresh shrimp
½ teaspoon salt
1 cup regular grits
2 large eggs, lightly beaten

¼ cup milk
2 cloves garlic, minced (optional)
1 ½ cups (6 ounces) shredded
    cheddar cheese, divided
Garnish: chopped fresh
    parsley

Bring 5 cups water to a boil in a large saucepan over high heat. Add shrimp and cook 3 minutes; drain. Rinse shrimp in cold water; peel and devein shrimp; set aside. Bring 3 ¼ cups water and salt to boil in a saucepan. Stir in grits; cover, reduce heat and cook until liquid is absorbed. Combine eggs and milk; stir a very small amount of grits into egg mixture to warm (to avoid curdling the eggs). Gradually stir egg mixture into grits. Stir in cooked shrimp, garlic and 1 cup of cheese. Spoon mixture into a lightly greased 11 x 7 x 1 ½-inch baking dish. Sprinkle with remaining ½ cup cheese. Bake at 350 degrees for 30 minutes; let stand 5 minutes. Garnish with parsley.

Yield: 6 servings

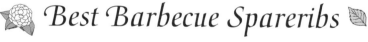

Best Barbecue Spareribs

6 pounds country style pork
    spareribs
4 teaspoons whole pickling spice
1 teaspoon salt
1 cup firmly packed lightly
    brown sugar

2 tablespoons dry mustard
½ cup ketchup
½ cola-flavored carbonated
    beverage

Place ribs in a large, deep pan. Cover with water. Add spice and salt. Bring mixture to a boil, reduce heat, and simmer for 45 minutes. Drain; sprinkle hot ribs with brown sugar and mustard. Cover and refrigerate 8 hours or overnight. Remove ribs from pan, reserving drippings. Combine drippings with ketchup and cola. Grill ribs 4 to 6 inches from coals for 30 to 45 minutes, basting frequently with cola mixture. If using a gas grill, cook over low heat.

Yield: 4 to 6 servings

Crab Cakes (Soul Food) ✓

1	large egg, lightly beaten	1	pound fresh crabmeat
2	tablespoons mayonnaise	3	tablespoons finely chopped
½	teaspoon dry mustard		fresh parsley
½	teaspoon salt	1½	tablespoons dry bread
½	teaspoon pepper		crumbs
¼	teaspoon hot pepper sauce		Vegetable oil for frying
⅛	teaspoon ground red pepper	1	lemon, cut into wedges

Whisk together egg, mayonnaise, mustard, salt, pepper, hot sauce and red pepper in a medium bowl. Stir in crab, parsley and bread crumbs. Shape into 8 equal portions about 2 to 2½ inches in diameter. Wrap in wax paper and refrigerate for 30 minutes. Fry in deep oil, 4 at a time, until golden brown. Drain on paper towels. Serve with tartar sauce.

Yield: 4 servings

Stuffed Crab in Shells ✓

2	tablespoons olive oil	6	saltines, crushed
3	stalks celery, diced	½	pound crabmeat
1	onion, diced	1	hard-cooked egg, chopped
¾	cup chili sauce		Salt
¼	teaspoon Worcestershire sauce		Pepper
1	large egg, lightly beaten	8	ceramic shells

Heat oil in a nonstick skillet over medium-high heat. Add celery and onion; sauté until tender. Pour into a mixing bowl; let cool. Stir chili sauce, Worcestershire and egg into celery mixture. Fold in crackers, crabmeat and egg; mix lightly until blended. Season to taste with salt and pepper. Spoon mixture evenly into shells and place shells in a shallow roasting pan. Pour water in pan to cover bottom of pan. Bake at 350 degrees until slightly browned.

Yield: 8 servings

Capa Cafe Crab Quiche

3   (9-inch) unbaked deep-dish pie shells
1 ½ cups (6 ounces) diced Swiss cheese
4 ½ cups (18 ounces) shredded Monterey Jack cheese
6   tablespoons all-purpose flour
9   large eggs, lightly beaten

2   (12-ounce) cans evaporated milk
1   teaspoon salt
¼   teaspoon white pepper
    Dash nutmeg
12 ounces fresh or pasteurized crabmeat
2   tablespoons finely grated onion

Prick bottom and sides of pie shells with a fork. Bake at 425 degrees for 6 to 8 minutes; set aside. Combine cheeses and flour; set aside. Combine eggs, milk, salt, pepper and nutmeg in a large bowl, mixing well. Stir in cheese/flour mixture, crabmeat and onion. Spoon mixture evenly into prepared pie shells. Bake at 350 degrees for 50 to 60 minutes. Cool slightly before serving. Recipe may be baked for 40 minutes, cooled and frozen. When ready to serve, thaw slightly and bake, covered, for 20 minutes or until heated through.

Yield: 6 servings per pie

Frogmore Stew ✓

Allow at least ¾ pound shrimp, 1 ear of corn and 6 inches of sausage per person. Reserve stock to be frozen and used in a bouillabaisse or fish stew. Multiply amount of ingredients by number of people to be served.

3 stalks celery, chopped	Pepper
1 large onion, chopped	Hot smoked sausage, sliced
1 large bell pepper, chopped	1 ½-inch thick
2 tablespoons shrimp and crab	Fresh corn, broken in half
boil seasoning	Shrimp, raw and unpeeled
Salt	

Combine celery, onion, pepper, seasoning, salt and pepper in a large Dutch oven or soup pot. Pour in enough water to cover ingredients. Bring mixture to a boil; boil for 10 to 15 minutes. Add sausage; boil 10 minutes. Add corn; boil 5 to 10 minutes. Add shrimp; boil 2 to 3 minutes. Remove from heat. Cover and let stand 4 to 5 minutes. Drain in colander.

Yield: 5 to 105 servings

Benne Wafers

½ cup butter	1 teaspoon vanilla
1 cup firmly packed light brown	1 large egg, lightly beaten
sugar	1 cup unbleached all-purpose
¼ teaspoon salt	flour
¼ teaspoon baking soda	1 cup toasted sesame seeds

Beat butter at medium speed with an electric mixer about 2 minutes or until creamy. Gradually add sugar, salt, baking soda, vanilla and egg. Stir in flour, beating until smooth. Stir in sesame seeds. Drop the dough by tablespoons onto parchment lined or lightly greased baking sheets. Bake at 350 degrees for 8 to 9 minutes or until golden brown. Remove from oven and let cool 1 minute. Transfer the wafers to a wire rack to completely cool.

Yield: 3 dozen 3-inch wafers

Cheddar Cheese Straws

*An old-fashioned Low country favorite, Cheese Straws
will start any gathering off with a blast of delicious gusto.*

½ cup butter	1 teaspoon baking powder
2 cups (8 ounces) shredded sharp cheddar cheese	½ teaspoon salt
1 ½ cups all-purpose flour	¼ teaspoon cayenne pepper, or more if desired

Combine butter and cheese in a large mixing bowl; beat well at medium speed of an electric mixer. Combine flour, baking powder, salt and cayenne. Gradually add flour mixture to cheese mixture, mixing until dough is no longer crumbly. Shape mixture into a ball. Prepare dough with any of the following procedures and place on an ungreased baking sheet. Bake at 350 degrees for 15 minutes or until golden brown.

Method 1: Roll out the dough to about ¼ to ½-inch thickness and cut into ½-inch wide strips.

Method 2: Use a cookie gun to shape dough into straws following manufacturer's instructions.

Method 3: Roll dough into a cylinder about 2 to 2½ inches in diameter. Cut into ¼-inch slices. The dough slices easily if chilled.

The dough may be prepared ahead of time, wrapped in wax paper and stored in the refrigerator.

Yield: 4 dozen

Fresh Grits—Add fresh basil, 1 tablespoon to 4 cups of hot cooked grits and 1 tablespoon minced sun-dried tomatoes.

Baked Cheese Grits ✓

If available, stone-ground grits are more flavorful and nutritious than instant grits. Cold leftover grits are still delicious when sliced, fried in a little butter and served hot.

2	cups grits	2	tablespoons butter
2	cups (8 ounces) shredded cheddar cheese, divided	½	teaspoon garlic salt
		⅛	teaspoon paprika
2	large eggs, lightly beaten		

Cook grits according to package directions, stirring occasionally. (You may use leftover grits; mash fine with a fork.) Stir in 1 ½ cups cheese, blending well. Stir in eggs, butter and garlic salt. Spoon grits into a greased 1 ½-quart baking dish. Top with remaining cheese and sprinkle with paprika. Bake at 375 degrees for 20 minutes. This dish goes well with most main courses of seafood, chicken and pork.

Yield: 6 to 8 servings

Okra Pilau ✓

Okra is exotic eating for Yankees—Prolific staple in the south!

3	slices bacon, chopped	1	(16-ounce) can tomatoes, drained and chopped or 3 fresh tomatoes, peeled and quartered
2	cups sliced okra		
¾	cup chopped onion		
½	cup chopped green bell pepper		Pinch rosemary or thyme
¾	cup uncooked rice		Salt
2	cups chicken broth		

Cook bacon and okra in a 3-quart saucepan over medium-high heat until lightly browned. Stir in onion and bell pepper; cook 5 minutes or until vegetables are tender. Add rice, chicken broth, tomatoes, rosemary and salt. Bring to a boil, stirring once. Reduce heat, and simmer for 15 minutes or until rice is tender.

Yield: 6 to 8 servings

Note: ¼ to ½ pound crumbled sausage may be substituted for bacon. 1 (10-ounce) package frozen okra, thawed, may be substituted for fresh.

Shrimp Jambalaya

½ pound bacon, chopped
⅔ cups chopped celery
½ cup chopped onion
½ cup chopped green pepper
2 ½ cups chicken broth, divided
1 ½ cups ketchup
½ pound or 1 (½-inch) slice ham, chopped
2 tablespoons sugar

2 tablespoons chopped fresh parsley
1 teaspoon thyme
⅛ teaspoon cayenne pepper
1 bay leaf
Salt
⅓ cup cornstarch
1 ½-2 pounds peeled and deveined cooked shrimp

Cook bacon in a large skillet over medium-high heat until crisp; remove bacon and drain on paper towels. Add celery, onion and green pepper to bacon drippings; sauté over medium-high heat until onion is transparent. Combine 2 cups chicken broth and ketchup in a large soup pot. Stir in bacon, cooked vegetables, ham, sugar, parsley, thyme, cayenne, bay leaf and salt. Bring to a boil, reduce heat to low, and simmer for 2 hours, stirring occasionally. Stir cornstarch into ½ cup cold chicken broth. Stir cornstarch into jambalaya. Cook over low heat 2 to 3 minutes until thickened. Stir in shrimp; cook over low heat for 10 minutes.

Yield: 4 servings

Note: For 8 servings, double the recipe. Prepare the day before, and add cornstarch just before placing in a serving dish. Keep warm in a 200 degree oven. Can be kept warm in oven up to two hours along with cooked rice. Remove from oven minutes before serving and add shrimp. Replace pot in oven while setting up buffet. Do not double the amount of shrimp.

Lemon juice rubbed on fish before cooking will enhance the flavor and help maintain a good color.

COOKIN' LOW COUNTRY

Clam Chowder

2	dozen medium hard-shelled clams		Salt
4	slices bacon, chopped		Freshly ground pepper
1	onion, chopped	1	cup milk
2	large potatoes, diced	½	cup light cream

Scrub clams to remove sand. Place 4 or 5 clams in a microwave-safe covered baking dish with about 2 tablespoons water. Microwave on HIGH for 3 to 4 minutes until shells open. Remove clams from shells, reserving liquid in a separate container. Repeat with remaining clams. Clean and chop clams. Strain clam liquid. You should have 3 cups clam juice. (You can refrigerate the clams and juice for a day until you are ready to prepare the chowder.) Cook bacon in a deep saucepan over medium-high heat until crisp. Add onion and sauté until golden brown. Stir in potatoes and clam juice. Bring mixture to a boil, reduce heat, and simmer until potatoes are tender. Stir in chopped clams; simmer 10 minutes. Season to taste with salt and pepper. Remove from heat. Heat milk and cream in a small saucepan over medium heat. Stir milk mixture gradually into chowder. Serve with crackers.

Yield: 6 servings

Eggplant and Okra Stew

This unusual combination of beef, fish and vegetables is found to be novel and delicious. This is a traditional Ghana dish that's made its way to the Low Country, especially if you season it with any kind of hot sauce.

½	pound beef, cut into small cubes	1	teaspoon tomato paste
12	eggplants, peeled and diced	8	pods okra, chopped or sliced (fresh or frozen)
1	cup vegetable oil	1	pound grilled or sautéed mackerel, boned and sliced
1	large sweet onion	¼	teaspoon white pepper
2	large tomatoes, peeled, seeded and chopped		Salt

Cook beef in a small amount of boiling, salted water until tender. Drain, reserving liquid, and set aside. Cook eggplants in a small amount of boiling, salted water until tender. Drain and set aside. Heat oil in a large soup pot over medium-high heat; add onion and sauté until tender. Add tomatoes and cook until liquid evaporates. Stir in tomato paste and okra. Cook, covered, for 3 to 5 minutes. Stir in beef liquid. Bring mixture to a boil, reduce heat to low, and cook until okra is tender. Add eggplant, beef, mackerel, white pepper and salt. Cook over low heat 15 to 20 minutes until stew thickens. Serve hot with boiled rice, potatoes, fried or boiled sweet potatoes or bananas.

Yield: 4 to 6 servings

---

*The kitchen is a mystical place
where the sounds and odors carry meaning
that transfers from the past and
bridges into the future.*

Baked Grits and Sausage Casserole

1 cup grits
1 pound bulk sausage
1 cup chopped onions
1 cup chopped celery
½ cup chopped green and red bell peppers

1 (10¾-ounce) can cream of celery soup
1 cup (4 ounces) shredded cheddar cheese

Cook grits according to package directions; season to taste with salt. Place in a large bowl; set aside. Brown sausage in a large skillet over medium-high heat, stirring until it crumbles; drain well. Stir into grits; set aside. Add onion, celery and pepper to same skillet; sauté over medium-high heat for 5 minutes. Stir onion mixture into grits mixture. Spoon into a lightly greased 2-quart baking dish. Spread celery soup over mixture and top evenly with cheese. Bake at 375 degrees for 30 minutes.

Yield: 6 servings

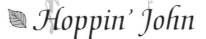 Hoppin' John

2	cups dried cow peas (black-eyed peas)	1	cup uncooked rice
4	slices bacon		Salt
1	small sweet onion, chopped		Pepper

Cook peas according to package direction until tender; do not drain. Cook bacon and onion in a large skillet until bacon is crisp. Remove bacon strips and drain on paper towels. Add cooked onion and 2 tablespoons of bacon drippings to the peas. Rinse rice and stir into pea mixture, adding more water, if necessary. Bring to a boil, reduce heat to low, and cook for 1 hour or until rice is fluffy. Season to taste with salt and pepper. Crumble bacon and stir into Hoppin' John just before serving.

Yield: 4 to 6 servings

Southern Beaten Biscuits

4	cups all-purpose flour	½	cup shortening, cut into pieces
1	teaspoon salt		Cold water

Combine flour and salt in a large bowl. Cut in shortening with a pastry blender or fork until mixture resembles a coarse meal. Stir in enough cold water to make a very stiff dough (so stiff that you feel almost hopeless of ever doing anything with it). Turn dough out onto a lightly floured surface. Beat with a wooden mallet until smooth and full of air bubbles. Roll dough to ¾-inch thickness; cut with a 2-inch round biscuit cutter and place on a lightly greased baking sheet. Pierce biscuits with a fork. Bake at 325 degrees for 30 minutes.

"Two hundred licks is what I gives
For home-folks never fewer:
And if I'm 'specting company in
I gives five hundred sure."

Hilton Head Fruit Cake

*Do not attempt this recipe in the privacy of your
home unless attended by a doctor and EMS is standing
nearby with the ambulance ready to go.*

1	cup water	2	cups dried fruit
1	cup firmly packed light brown sugar	1	cup sugar
		8	ounces nuts
1	teaspoon salt	1	teaspoon soda
1	large bottle rum		Juice of one lemon
4	large eggs		

Taste the rum to check quality. Take a large bowl. Sample the rum again to be sure it's the highest quality--pour 1 level cup and drink. Repeat. Turn on the electric mixer, beat 1 cup of butter in a large fluffy bowl. Add 1 teaspoon soda and beat bowl again. Turn off the mixer. Chuck in the dried fruit, break 2 eggs and add bowl. Mix on the turnerer. If the fried fruit sticks in beaters, pry loose with a drewscriver. Sample the rum to check the tonsisticity. Then sift 2 cups of salt. Or something. Who cares? Check the rum. Now strain the nuts and sift the lemon juice. Add 1 table. Spoon sugar on something. Whatever you can find. Grease the oven. Preheat the cake tin to 350 degrees. Don't forget to beat off the turner. Throw the bowl out of the window, taste the rum and go to bed!

Yield: Who cares?

---

*Abstinence is a good
thing if practiced in moderation.*

Soups, Salads & Sandwiches

Folks will flock to your table for soups, salads and sandwiches. Always a crowd pleaser, soups, salads and sandwiches fit any schedule, satisfying the hungriest gang of guests, still giving you time, when prepared ahead, to relax and enjoy the party.

The *Soups, Salads and Sandwiches* photo shows a flock of hungry Wood Storks stirring up dinner with their huge feet; their sharp 9 ½ inch beaks snapping up fish, crayfish and snakes which float to the top of the tidal lagoon in Moss Creek Plantation. The Wood Stork, formerly known as the Wood Ibis, is the only American stork. Wood Storks have also been called "Preachers" for their habit of standing on the bank with heads and beaks down so low to their chests that they appear to be praying. It's thought they may be aiding digestion by this position.

Twice Treasured Recipes won't, in this or any other section, serve up snake, but we can help you stir up a zesty soup served with a palate-tickling salad and scrumptious sandwiches to feed your hungry flock. Your folks may not digest their meals standing up, but they may be heard praying for another meal of our *Soups, Salads and Sandwiches.*

Soups, Salads & Sandwiches

Soups, Salads & Sandwiches

🌺 **Quick and Easy Recipes are designated with a camellia flower.**
🍃 **Memorable Menu Recipes are designated with a leaf.**

Clam Chowder

Delicious with corn muffins.

1 small onion	1 cup cooked clams and broth
½ cup coarsely chopped celery	1 (3-ounce) package cream
1 tablespoon vegetable oil	cheese
3 cups milk	1 teaspoon dried parsley
3 cups very finely chopped	Salt
potatoes	Pepper

Combine onion and celery in a food processor; process until finely minced. Heat oil in a skillet over medium-high heat. Add onion and carrot; sauté until tender. Stir in milk, potatoes, clams and broth, cream cheese, parsley, salt and pepper. Cook over low heat, stirring frequently, until cream cheese is melted and chowder is thoroughly heated.

Yield: 6 to 8 servings

 # Chili

¾-1 pound lean ground beef	3 tablespoons chili powder
2 tablespoons instant minced	1 tablespoon all-purpose flour
onion	1 tablespoon sugar
1 (16-ounce) can kidney beans,	1 teaspoon salt
rinsed and drained	3 tablespoons water
3-4 cups tomato juice	

Brown ground beef and onion in a large skillet over medium-high heat, stirring until it crumbles; drain if desired. Stir in beans and tomato juice; cook 10 minutes. Combine chili powder, flour, sugar and salt in a small bowl; add water, stirring to make a paste. Stir into beef mixture. Cook over low heat, stirring occasionally, for 30 minutes.

Yield: 6 servings

Broccoli-Cheese Soup

¼ cup butter, divided	2 tablespoons all-purpose flour
1 large onion, chopped	1 cup milk
1 ½-2 cups water	½-1 cup (2 to 4 ounces) shredded cheddar cheese
2-3 beef bouillon cubes	1-2 cooked potatoes, cubed
1 bunch (1 pound) fresh broccoli, cut into florets	2 tablespoons sherry (optional)

Melt 2 tablespoons butter in a medium saucepan over medium-high heat; add onion and sauté until tender. Add water, bouillon and broccoli. Bring mixture to a boil, reduce heat, and simmer until broccoli is tender. Melt 2 tablespoons butter in large saucepan over medium heat; add flour, whisking until smooth. Cook 1 minute, whisking constantly. Gradually add milk; cook, whisking constantly, until mixture is thickened and bubbly. Stir in Cheese. Add broccoli mixture, potatoes and sherry. Cook, stirring constantly, until soup thickens. Season to taste with salt and pepper. Serve piping hot.

Yield: 4 servings

SOUPS, SALADS, & SANDWICHES

Creamy Carrot Soup

3 tablespoons butter	Hot pepper sauce or Cajun
1 cup chopped onion	seasoning
1 ½ pounds carrots, peeled and	2 (10 ¾-ounce) cans cream of
sliced	potato soup
2 (16-ounce) cans chicken	2 tablespoons lemon juice
broth	1 ½ tablespoons honey
½ teaspoon dried tarragon	½ cup heavy whipping cream
½ teaspoon salt	Garnishes: sour cream,
½ teaspoon white pepper	chopped fresh parsley
⅛ teaspoon dried thyme	

Melt butter in a large saucepan over medium heat; sauté onion until translucent. Add carrots, chicken broth, tarragon, salt, white pepper and thyme. Add hot sauce to taste. Bring mixture to a boil, reduce heat, and simmer 10 minutes or until carrots are tender. Stir in potato soup, lemon juice and honey. Pour soup in batches in a blender; cover top with towel to reduce splashing. Process until very smooth. Pour soup into a large bowl after each batch; cover and chill 8 hours or overnight. Stir in heavy cream. Thin soup with milk if necessary. To serve, garnish with a dollop of sour cream and sprinkle with parsley.

Yield: 6 to 8 servings

A lettuce leaf dropped into the pot absorbs the grease from the top of the soup. Remove the lettuce and throw it away as soon as it has served its purpose.

Curried Butternut Squash Soup

The rich flavor and smooth texture of this low-fat soup comes from pureeing the soup in batches. The soup freezes well and there is no need to thaw before reheating. When ready to serve, simply reheat from frozen state.

3	tablespoons margarine or butter, divided	2	(14 ½-ounce) cans chicken broth
2	large onions, sliced	½	teaspoon salt
1	tablespoon curry powder	2 ¼	cups water
2	large butternut squashes (3 ½ pounds total), peeled, seeded and cut into ½-inch pieces		

Melt 2 tablespoon margarine in a 5-quart saucepan or Dutch oven over medium heat. Add onions and sauté 18 to 20 minutes, stirring occasionally, until golden brown. Stir in curry and remaining tablespoon of margarine; cook 1 minute, stirring constantly. Stir in squash, broth, salt and 2 ¼ cups water. Bring mixture to a boil, reduce heat to low; cover and simmer for 20 minutes or until squash is very tender. Pour soup in batches in a blender; cover top with towel to reduce splashing. Process until very smooth. Pour soup into a large bowl after each batch. Return soup to saucepan; cook until thoroughly heated.

Yield: 12 first-course servings

A home is a place where a pot of fresh soup simmers gently, filling the kitchen with soft aromas, filling your heart and later your tummy with joy.

SOUPS, SALADS, & SANDWICHES

Corn and Shrimp Chowder ✓✓

Make this creamy chowder ahead. Prepare the soup as directed, omitting the shrimp. Refrigerate up to 2 days or freeze up to 1 month. Reheat the soup over low heat. Stir in the shrimp and cook 5 minutes until tender.

1 ¾ pounds medium shrimp	2 (14 ½-ounce) cans chicken broth
1 tablespoon butter or margarine	2 teaspoons sugar
1 tablespoon olive oil	½ teaspoon salt
3 carrots, peeled and coarsely chopped	½ teaspoon dried thyme
	⅛- ¼ teaspoon cayenne pepper
1 large onion, coarsely chopped	2 cups of water
1 stalk celery, coarsely chopped	½ cup half-and-half or light cream
2 (10-ounce) packages frozen whole-kernel corn	Garnish: chopped fresh thyme

Shell and devein 20 shrimp, leaving tail on (for garnish). Shell and devein remaining shrimp; slice each in half horizontally. Cover and refrigerate until ready to prepare. Heat butter and oil in a 5-quart saucepan or Dutch oven over medium heat. Add carrots, onion and celery. Sauté for 15 minutes, stirring often, until vegetables are tender. Set aside 1 ½ cups corn. Stir remaining corn into saucepan. Stir in chicken broth, sugar, salt, thyme, cayenne and 2 cups water. Bring mixture to a boil, reduce heat to low; simmer, covered, for 20 minutes, stirring occasionally. Pour water to a depth of 2 inches in a 2-quart saucepan over high heat. Bring to a boil; add the 20 shrimp with tails. Cook 1 minute or until shrimp are done. Drain and keep warm. Pour soup in batches in a blender; cover top with towel to reduce splashing. Process until very smooth. Pour soup into a large bowl after each batch. Return soup to saucepan; stir in reserved corn. Stir in half-and-half. Heat soup over medium heat until hot, stirring occasionally. (Do not boil.) Add sliced shrimp and cook 5 minutes or until shrimp are done. To serve, spoon chowder into 10 bowls; garnish each with 2 whole shrimp. Sprinkle with thyme.

Yield: 10 first-course servings

Hot Apple and Bourbon Soup

1 tablespoon olive oil (more if necessary)	1 tablespoon fresh ginger, peeled and chopped
6 large or 8 medium apples, peeled, cored and chopped	1 cup bourbon
4 carrots, peeled and chopped	4 cloves garlic, minced
2 red onions, finely chopped	4 cups water
½ large leek, rinsed well and chopped	2 cups heavy whipping cream Salt

Heat oil in a large saucepan over medium heat. Add apples, carrots, onions, leek and ginger; sauté for 10 minutes. Stir in bourbon. Bring mixture to a boil, reduce heat, and simmer 20 minutes until liquid is reduced by one-third. Stir in garlic and water. Bring to a boil, reduce heat, and simmer until vegetables are tender. Pour soup in batches in a blender; cover top with towel to reduce splashing. Process until very smooth. Pour soup into a large bowl after each batch and stir in cream. Transfer soup to saucepan and reheat, if necessary. (Do not boil.) Serve hot.

Yield: 8 to 10 servings

"Free Soup"—to save money and vitamins: Pour all leftover vegetables and water they are cooked in, into a freezer container. When the container is full, add tomato juice, seasoning and have "free soup" for lunch.

Emerald Spinach Soup ✓

5	tablespoons unsalted butter		Ground nutmeg (optional)
¼	pound fresh mushrooms, trimmed and diced	½	(8-ounce) package cream cheese, cubed
1	green onion, chopped	1	cup (4 ounces) shredded Swiss cheese (Jarlsberg recommended)
5	tablespoons all-purpose flour		
2	cups chicken broth		
2	cups milk	¾	pound fresh spinach, washed, cooked and chopped
½	teaspoon salt (optional)		
	Fresh ground pepper		

Melt butter in a large saucepan over medium heat. Add mushrooms and green onion; sauté until tender. Add flour, whisking until well blended. Cook 1 to 2 minutes, whisking constantly. Gradually add broth and milk; cook over medium heat, whisking constantly, until mixture is thickened and bubbly. Add salt, pepper, nutmeg, cream cheese and Swiss cheese; stir until well blended and cheeses melt. Stir in spinach; cook until thoroughly heated, stirring gently. Season to taste with salt and pepper. Serve hot.

Yield: 4 to 6 servings

√ # *Mulligatawny Soup*

¼ cup butter
1 onion, sliced
1 carrot, peeled and sliced
1 green bell pepper, sliced
1 stalk celery, sliced
1 tart apple, peeled, cored and sliced
1 cup chopped cooked chicken
¼ cup all-purpose flour
1 teaspoon curry powder or more, to taste

2 whole cloves
1 parsley sprig, minced
Pinch nutmeg
2 (14¾-ounce) cans chicken broth
1 (16-ounce) can whole tomatoes, chopped
Salt
Freshly ground pepper

Melt butter over medium heat in a large saucepan. Add onion, carrot, bell pepper, celery, apple and chicken. Sauté 10 minutes or until vegetables are tender. Add flour, curry powder, cloves, parsley and nutmeg, stirring until well blended. Cook 1 minute, stirring constantly. Gradually add broth, tomatoes with liquid, salt and pepper; cook over medium-low heat 30 minutes or until mixture is thickened and bubbly. Discard cloves.

Yield: 6 servings

Shoppers overheard while in line at The Bargain Box:

"If it isn't at The Bargain Box my kids don't need it!"

"If there's anything better than The Bargain Box, God must be keeping it to himself."

Gazpacho √√

1 quart tomato juice	⅓ cup olive oil
2 (10 ½-ounce) cans beef consommé	3 tablespoons lime juice
	1 tablespoon lemon juice
6 large tomatoes, peeled, seeded and chopped	1 tablespoon honey
	1 teaspoon salt
2 onions, chopped	1 teaspoon dried tarragon
2 cucumbers, seeded and chopped	1 teaspoon dried basil
	½ teaspoon pepper
2 shallots, chopped	Garlic salt
1 green bell pepper, chopped	Hot pepper sauce
1 red bell pepper, chopped	Garnishes: sour cream, fresh dill weed
¼ cup fresh parsley, minced	
½ cup red wine vinegar	

Celery

Combine juice, consommé, tomatoes, onions, cucumbers, shallots, bell peppers, parsley, vinegar, oil, juices, honey, salt, tarragon, basil and pepper in a large bowl. Season to taste with garlic salt and pepper sauce. Cover and refrigerate until well chilled. Garnish each serving with a dollop of sour cream and a sprinkle of fresh dill.

Yield: 8 to 12 servings

SOUPS, SALADS, & SANDWICHES

Potage Parmentier

*If you can't find leeks—use yellow onions. Believe it or not . . .
you really can't tell the difference. This soup is even more
delicious when made a day ahead.*

3	cups thinly sliced leeks or yellow onions	1-2	teaspoons salt
4	cups peeled, diced potatoes	½	cup heavy whipping cream
2	quarts chicken stock		Garnish: chopped fresh parsley

Soak leeks in water to remove all grit; drain. Combine leeks, potato, chicken stock and salt in a large saucepan. Bring mixture to a boil, reduce heat, and simmer for 45 to 50 minutes until vegetables are tender. Pour soup in batches in a blender or food processor; cover top with towel to reduce splashing. Process until very smooth. Pour soup into a large bowl after each batch. Transfer soup to saucepan and reheat, if necessary. Stir in cream just before serving; garnish with parsley and serve hot.

Yield: 12 servings

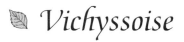 Vichyssoise

This easy soup is great for winter or summer.

1	recipe Potage Parmentier	Salt
1	cup heavy whipping cream	Garnish: minced fresh chives

Combine soup and cream in a large bowl. Cover and refrigerate at least 2 hours until well chilled. Season to taste with salt. Serve in chilled soup cups and garnish with chives.

Yield: 12 servings

Tortellini Bean Soup

2 tablespoons olive oil	1 (16-ounce) can kidney beans, rinsed and drained
1 onion, chopped	
2 large cloves garlic, minced	¼ teaspoon dried basil
¼ pound sliced prosciutto, chopped (not shaved)	¼ teaspoon dried oregano
	¼ teaspoon pepper
6 cups chicken broth	1 (10-ounce) package frozen chopped spinach, thawed and drained
1 (28-ounce) can diced tomatoes	
2 (9-ounce) packages refrigerated cheese tortellini	¼ cup freshly grated Romano cheese

Heat oil in a 4-quart saucepan over medium heat. Add onion, garlic and prosciutto; sauté 5 minutes. Stir in broth, tomatoes, tortellini, beans, basil, oregano and pepper. Bring mixture to a boil, reduce heat, and simmer 5 minutes. Stir in spinach; cook until thoroughly heated. To serve, top each bowl with grated cheese.

Yield: 6 to 8 servings

 Tortilla Soup

1	(16-ounce) can chicken or beef broth	2	(10-ounce) cans chopped cooked chicken
1	(15 ½-ounce) can northern beans	1	(16-ounce) package frozen whole kernel corn
1	(15 ½-ounce) can pinto beans	1	(1-ounce) envelope taco seasoning mix
1	(14 ½-ounce) can diced tomatoes	1	(1-ounce) envelope buttermilk salad dressing mix
1	(14 ½-ounce) can diced tomatoes with green chiles		Sliced tortillas or tortilla chips
1	(12-ounce) can tomato juice		Shredded cheddar cheese
1	(4 ½-ounce) can diced green chiles		

Combine broth, beans, tomatoes, tomatoes with chiles, juice, chiles, chicken, corn, seasoning mix and dressing mix in a large saucepan over medium-high heat. Stir in water to desired consistency. Bring mixture to a boil, reduce heat, and simmer 30 minutes. Stir tortillas into each serving and top with cheese, or serve tortillas on the side.

Yield: 10 to 12 servings

Note: 3 to 4 cooked and sliced chicken breasts or 1 pound cooked and drained ground beef may be substituted for canned chicken. 1 jar of commercial salsa may be substituted for tomatoes with diced green chiles and diced green chiles.

Yankee Bean Soup

3	tablespoons vegetable oil	1	(16-ounce) can whole
½	pound ham, cut into		tomatoes, drained and
	¼-inch cubes		chopped
1 ½	cups chopped onion		Dried thyme
½	cup chopped celery		Dried basil
½	cup chopped carrots		Ground coriander
4	cups chicken broth		Ground cumin
2	(16-ounce) cans black, pinto		Pepper
	or navy beans		

Heat oil in a large saucepan over medium-high heat. Add ham, onion, celery and carrots; sauté 10 minutes until onion is tender. Stir in broth, beans and tomatoes. Bring mixture to a boil, reduce heat, and simmer 30 minutes. Season to taste with thyme, basil, coriander, cumin and pepper.

Yield: 6 servings

Onion Soup with Parmesan Croutons

Slow-cooking onions, shallots and leeks will caramelize their natural sugars and add a sweet, rich flavor to this classic soup. The soup can be made the day ahead and reheated. The croutons can be made up to 2 days ahead if stored in an airtight container.

10	(¾-inch thick) slices French bread	3	large onions, halved and thinly sliced
¼	cup coarsely grated Parmesan cheese		Pinch dried thyme
1	bunch leeks (about 1 pound)	2	tablespoons brandy
2	tablespoons butter or margarine	3	(14¼-ounce) cans chicken broth
1	tablespoon olive oil	1	teaspoon salt
4	large shallots, halved and thinly sliced	¼	teaspoon coarse ground pepper
		4	cups water

Place bread slices on a baking sheet. Bake at 450 degrees for 3 minutes. Turn slices over; sprinkle evenly with Parmesan cheese and bake 5 minutes. Set aside. Cut the roots from leeks and discard tough outer leaves. Cut each leek in half lengthwise. Rinse thoroughly with cold running water to remove grit. Slice leeks crosswise into ¼-inch pieces. Soak in water to remove all grit; drain and set aside. Heat butter and oil in an 8-quart saucepan over medium-high heat; add leeks, shallots, onions and thyme. Cook, covered, 40 to 45 minutes, stirring occasionally, until tender and deep golden brown. Remove cover and increase heat to high. Add brandy and cook 1 minute, stirring and scraping bottom of saucepan. Stir in broth, salt, pepper and 4 cups of water. Bring mixture to a boil, reduce heat to low, and simmer 20 minutes. Top each serving of soup with a Parmesan crouton.

Yield: 10 servings

Vegetable Chowder ✓

2	cups peeled and diced potatoes	1 ½	tablespoons Worcestershire sauce
¾	cup minced onion	½	teaspoon pepper
1	cup chopped celery	1	(14 ½-ounce) can diced tomatoes, drained
2 ½	teaspoons salt	3	cups (12 ounces) shredded sharp cheddar cheese
2 ½	cups water		Garnish: chopped fresh parsley
¼	cup butter		
¼	cup all-purpose flour		
2	cups milk		
½	cup sherry (optional)		

Combine potatoes, onion, celery, salt and water in a medium saucepan. Bring mixture to a boil, reduce heat, and simmer 15 minutes or until vegetables are tender. Do not drain. Melt butter in a large saucepan over medium heat; add flour, whisking until smooth. Cook 1 minute, whisking constantly. Gradually add milk; cook, whisking constantly, until mixture is thickened and bubbly. Stir in sherry, Worcestershire sauce and pepper. Stir vegetable mixture into white sauce. Add tomatoes and grated cheese, stirring until well blended. Garnish each serving with parsley.

Yield: 4 servings

 If your recipe calls for diced bacon, it's best to cut it while still semi-frozen.

Yellow Pepper Soup

This soup keeps well refrigerated up to
2 days. Reheat, and check seasonings before serving.

1 large slice Italian bread	2¾ cups homemade or
4 leeks	low-sodium canned
2 tablespoons olive oil	chicken broth
6 yellow bell peppers	Salt
(2 pounds), seeded and cut	Freshly ground pepper
into pieces	Garnish: fresh tarragon
6 large sprigs of tarragon	leaves, olive oil

Slice bread into 8, ½ x 3-inch pieces. Toast until golden brown; set aside. Cut the roots from leeks and discard tough outer leaves. Cut each leek in half lengthwise. Rinse thoroughly with cold running water to remove grit. Slice leeks crosswise into ¼-inch pieces, using the white and light green parts only. Soak in water to remove all grit; drain and set aside. Heat oil in a small soup pot over low heat. Add leeks and sauté 10 minutes or until wilted. Stir in peppers, tarragon, broth, salt and pepper. Bring mixture to a boil, reduce heat, and simmer 20 minutes or until peppers are tender. Remove from heat; discard tarragon sprigs. Pour soup in batches in a blender or food processor; cover top with towel to reduce splashing. Process until very smooth. Pass the puree through a fine mesh strainer and adjust seasoning with salt and pepper, if necessary. Divide the soup among 4 bowls and top each with 2 of the toast pieces. Garnish with tarragon leaves; drizzle with olive oil. Serve immediately.

Yield: 4 servings

 # *Vegetable Soup*

½	head cabbage, cut into large pieces	1	(10-ounce) package frozen French-style green beans, thawed
2	cups water, divided		Salt
1	(10-ounce) package frozen chopped spinach, thawed		Pepper
1	(10-ounce) package frozen cauliflower florets, thawed	5	teaspoons chicken bouillon granules
1	(10-ounce) package cut broccoli, thawed	½	teaspoon onion powder

Place half of cabbage pieces in a blender with 1 cup of water; process until finely chopped. Repeat with remaining cabbage and water. (You may also process cabbage in a food processor with no water. Add the 2 cups water to the remaining ingredients.) Place cabbage with water in a large saucepan. Stir in spinach, cauliflower, broccoli, green beans, salt and pepper. Bring mixture to a boil, reduce heat, and simmer 10 minutes or until vegetables are tender. Stir in bouillon and onion powder. Cook, stirring often, until bouillon dissolves.

Yield: 6 servings

Zesty Pumpkin Soup

¼	cup butter	⅛	teaspoon crushed red pepper flakes
1	cup chopped onion	3	cups chicken broth
1	clove garlic, crushed	1	(16-ounce) can solid pack
1	teaspoon curry powder		pumpkin
½	teaspoon salt	1	cup half-and-half
⅛-¼	teaspoon ground coriander		Garnish: sour cream, chives

Melt butter in a large saucepan over medium heat. Add onion and garlic; sauté until tender. Stir in curry powder, salt, coriander and pepper flakes; cook 1 minute. Stir in broth. Bring mixture to a boil, reduce heat, and simmer for 15 to 20 minutes. Stir in pumpkin and half-and-half; cook 5 minutes over medium heat. Pour soup in batches in a blender; cover top with towel to reduce splashing. Process until very smooth. Pour soup into a large bowl after each batch and stir in cream. Transfer soup to saucepan and reheat, if necessary. (Do not boil.) Garnish with a dollop of sour cream and chopped chives.

Yield: 6 cups

White Chili

1 ½-2	pounds ground chicken or turkey	1	(48-ounce) can great Northern beans, undrained
1	(16-ounce) can chicken broth	1	(8-ounce) package shredded Monterey Jack cheese with peppers
1	(16-ounce) jar mild or medium salsa		
		2	teaspoons ground cumin

Brown chicken in a 5-quart Dutch oven or saucepan over medium-high heat, stirring until it crumbles. Stir in chicken broth, salsa, beans, cheese and cumin. Simmer over medium-low heat for 1 hour.

Yield: 8 servings

SOUPS, SALADS, & SANDWICHES

Turkey Chili

2	pounds ground turkey	¾	teaspoon dried oregano
2	(14 ½-ounce) cans diced tomatoes	½	teaspoon pepper
2	(16-ounce) cans red kidney beans, drained	½	teaspoon ground cinnamon
		¼- ½	teaspoon ground red pepper
1	(8-ounce) can tomato sauce	1	clove garlic, minced
½	cup chopped onions	1	bay leaf
¼	cup red wine or chicken broth		Garnish: yellow or green pepper rings
¾	teaspoon dried basil		

Brown turkey in a large saucepan, stirring until it crumbles; drain. Stir in tomatoes, beans, sauce, onions, broth, basil, oregano, pepper, cinnamon, red pepper, garlic and bay leaf. Bring mixture to a boil, reduce heat, and simmer, covered, for 2 hours stirring occasionally. Remove bay leaf and garnish with pepper rings. Serve over rice or on hamburger buns. Recipe freezes well; reheat on stove.

Yield: 6 servings

Cold Cucumber Soup

3	cucumbers, peeled and coarsely chopped	1	small onion, grated
2	cups sour cream	2	tablespoons white wine vinegar
1	(14 ½-ounce) can chicken broth	1	clove garlic, crushed

Place cucumbers in a blender; process until pureed. Add sour cream and broth; process slowly until well blended. Add onion, vinegar and garlic. Process 1 minute until blended. Transfer soup to a bowl; cover and refrigerate until well chilled.

Yield: 6 to 8 servings

Zucchini and Sausage Soup

1	pound sweet Italian sausage	1	teaspoon dried oregano
2	cups celery, cut into ½-inch pieces	1	teaspoon sugar
		¼	teaspoon garlic powder
6	cups zucchini (2 pounds), cut into ½-inch pieces	½	teaspoon dried basil
		2	green bell peppers, chopped
2	(28-ounce) cans tomatoes	1	can beef broth, optional
1	cup chopped onion		Salt
1	teaspoon Italian seasoning		Pepper

Remove sausage from casings and coarsely chop. Brown sausage in a large saucepan over medium-high heat until browned; drain well. Add celery and cook 10 minutes, stirring often. Stir in zucchini, tomatoes, onion, Italian seasoning, oregano, sugar, garlic powder and basil. Bring mixture to a boil, reduce heat, and simmer 30 minutes. Stir in peppers; cook 10 minutes. Add 1 can of beef broth if more liquid is needed. Season to taste with salt and pepper.

Yield: 6 servings

Carrot Salad

5	cups sliced carrots	1	onion, chopped
1	(10¾-ounce) can tomato soup	1	teaspoon pepper
1	cup sugar	1	teaspoon salt
¾	cup white vinegar	1	teaspoon prepared mustard
½	cup salad oil	1	teaspoon Worcestershire sauce
1	green bell pepper, chopped		

Cook carrots in boiling water until tender; drain and cool. Combine soup, sugar, vinegar, oil, bell pepper, onion, pepper, salt, mustard and Worcestershire sauce in a large bowl. Add carrots, stirring gently until coated. Cover and refrigerate until well chilled.

Yield: 8 servings

Zucchini Soup

Can be served cold.

6	small zucchini, cubed or shredded	2	tablespoons fresh herbs (a combination of oregano, basil, parsley and chives)
2	tablespoons butter		
1	tablespoon vegetable oil	2	tablespoons lemon juice
2	onions, finely minced		Salt
1	clove garlic, minced		Pepper
5	cups chicken broth		

Place zucchini in a colander, sprinkle with salt and allow to drain for 10 minutes. Heat butter and oil in a large soup pot over medium-high heat. Add onions and garlic; sauté until onions are golden brown. Dry zucchini on paper towels; add to onions and cook over low heat for 5 minutes. Stir in chicken broth. Bring mixture to a boil, reduce heat, and simmer 15 minutes. Pour soup in batches in a blender; cover top with towel to reduce splashing. Process until very smooth. Transfer soup to saucepan. Stir in herbs and lemon juice; season to taste with salt and pepper. Reheat and serve. Can be served cold.

Yield: 6 to 8 servings

Black Bean Luau Salad

1	(20-ounce) can pineapple chunks, drained	1	red or green bell pepper, chopped
1	(16-ounce) can black beans, rinsed and drained	½	cup chopped celery
		½	cup chopped green onion
1-1½	cups cooked brown or white rice	½	cup fat-free or light honey-mustard salad dressing
1½	cups cubed, cooked chicken breast		

Combine pineapple, beans, rice, chicken, bell pepper, celery and green onion in a large bowl. Stir in salad dressing, tossing to coat.

Yield: 8 servings

Chicken Salad Oriental

¼ cup butter or margarine	2 cups cubed, cooked chicken
1 ½ cups chopped celery	8 ounces cooked rotini pasta, well drained
½ cup chopped green onion	
1 (10 ¾-ounce) can cream of chicken soup	1 (8-ounce) can sliced water chestnuts, drained
½ cup mayonnaise	1 cup chow mein noodles
2 tablespoons soy sauce	

Melt butter in a large skillet over medium heat. Add celery and green onion; sauté until tender. Combine cooked vegetables, soup, mayonnaise, soy sauce, chicken, pasta and water chestnuts in a large bowl, stirring to blend. Spoon into a lightly greased 3-quart baking dish. Bake at 350 degrees for 20 minutes or until thoroughly heated. Sprinkle with chow mein noodles and bake 5 minutes.

Yield: 8 servings

Cauliflower Salad

1 (8-ounce) carton sour cream	1 large head cauliflower, separated into florets
1 (.65-ounce) envelope cheese-garlic salad dressing mix	1 (7-ounce) jar pimiento-stuffed olives, drained and halved
1 tablespoon vegetable oil	Lettuce leaves
1 tablespoon lemon juice	Garnish: paprika

Combine sour cream, dressing mix, oil and lemon juice in a large bowl. Add cauliflower and olives, tossing to coat. Serve salad on lettuce leaves and garnish with paprika.

Yield: 8 to 10 servings

Chicken Avocado Salad

4	boneless, skinless chicken breasts	8	slices bacon, cooked crisp and broken into 1-inch pieces
2	cups diced avocado		Blue Cheese Dressing
¼	cup fresh lemon juice		Garnish: tomato wedges
½	teaspoon salt		
1	head romaine lettuce, torn into 2-inch pieces		

Poach chicken breasts in slowly boiling water for 7 to 10 minutes or until done. Cut into 1 ½-inch pieces; set aside. Combine warm chicken, avocado, lemon juice and salt in a bowl, tossing gently to coat. Arrange lettuce in 4 salad bowls. Divide the chicken mixture evenly among the bowls. Sprinkle bacon pieces on top. Garnish with tomato wedges and serve with blue cheese dressing.

Yield: 4 servings

Blue Cheese Dressing:

1	cup mayonnaise	2 ½	tablespoons crumbled blue cheese
⅓	cup chicken broth		Freshly ground pepper
½	cup sour cream	¼	cup fresh lemon juice

Combine mayonnaise, broth, sour cream, blue cheese, pepper and ¼ cup juice in a medium bowl; cover and chill until serving.

Yield: 2 cups

Chicken Salad Carlotta

4 boneless, skinless chicken breasts	2 tablespoons low-fat sour cream
1 cup chicken broth	2 ½ teaspoons curry powder
2 cups seedless green grapes	1 cup coarsely chopped fresh pineapple
½ cup golden raisins	
1 mango, peeled, seeded and cut into ½-inch cubes	1 cup mandarin orange segments
¾ cup low-fat yogurt	1 cup chopped almonds
¼ cup mango chutney	Mixed salad greens
¼ cup fresh minced Italian parsley	1 cup flaked coconut

Place chicken breast in a baking pan and cover with broth. Bake at 350 degrees for 25 to 30 minutes or until chicken is tender and juices run clear when pierced with a knife. Remove chicken; cool. Shred chicken into bite-size pieces in a large bowl. Stir in grapes, raisins and mango; mixing well. Combine yogurt, chutney, parsley, sour cream and curry powder in a small bowl. Stir into chicken mixture. Cover and refrigerate at least 3 hours. Stir in pineapple, oranges and almonds just before serving. Serve on a bed of mixed greens and sprinkle with coconut.

Yield: 6 servings

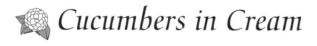 Cucumbers in Cream

2 cucumbers, peeled and thinly sliced	1 cup low-fat sour cream or yogurt
1 sweet onion, thinly sliced	¼ cup white wine vinegar
1 teaspoon salt	1 tablespoon sugar

Combine cucumber and onion in a large bowl; sprinkle with salt and let stand 10 minutes. Stir in sour cream, vinegar and sugar. Cover and refrigerate several hours until well chilled.

Yield: 6 to 8 servings

SOUPS, SALADS, & SANDWICHES

Frosted Polynesian Salad ✓

1 (10-ounce) package frozen peas, thawed	2 (4-ounce) cans sliced mushrooms, drained
1 head lettuce, chopped	1 ½ cups mayonnaise
2 green bell peppers, chopped	1 ½ cups sour cream
2 (8-ounce) cans sliced water chestnuts, drained	⅓ cup sugar
3 carrots, peeled and grated	3 cups (12 ounces) shredded cheddar cheese
2 (15-ounce) cans pineapple tidbits, drained	¾ pound bacon, cooked and crumbled

Cook peas slightly according to package directions; drain. Place chopped lettuce in 13 x 9 x 2-inch baking dish. Layer peas, bell peppers, water chestnuts, carrots, pineapple and mushrooms over lettuce. Combine mayonnaise, sour cream and sugar in a small bowl. Spread evenly over layered mixture. Cover with plastic wrap and refrigerate 8 hours or overnight. Two hours before serving, combine cheese and bacon; sprinkle over salad. Cut into squares and serve.

Yield: 12 servings

SOUPS, SALADS, & SANDWICHES

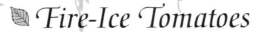

✓ Fire-Ice Tomatoes

6	large, ripe tomatoes, peeled and quartered
1	large green bell pepper, halved and sliced into strips
1	large red onion, sliced
¾	cup vinegar
4 ½	teaspoons sugar
1 ½	teaspoons celery salt

½	teaspoon mustard seed
½	teaspoon salt
⅛	teaspoon cayenne pepper
⅛	teaspoon pepper
¼	cup cold water
1	large cucumber, peeled and sliced

Arrange vegetables in separate sections in a large (nonmetal) baking dish or deep platter. Combine vinegar, sugar, celery salt, mustard seed, salt, cayenne pepper, pepper and cold water in a small saucepan. Bring to a boil; boil vigorously for 1 minute. Pour over vegetables; cool slightly. Cover and refrigerate until well chilled. Arrange cucumber with other vegetables just before serving.

Yield: 10 to 12 servings

Marinated Broccoli

1 ½	cups vegetable oil
1	cup apple cider vinegar
1	tablespoon dried dill weed
1	teaspoon salt

1	teaspoon garlic salt
1	teaspoon pepper
3	crowns broccoli, cut into florets

Combine oil, vinegar, dill, salt, garlic salt and pepper in a bowl. Add broccoli, tossing to coat. Cover and refrigerate at least 24 hours, stirring several times.

Yield: 10 to 12 servings

Healthy Chicken Salad

For an extra flavor boost, try the following method of preparing chicken for any chicken salad: Cut 4 to 6 carrots into 2-inch pieces and spread on the bottom of a large, shallow pan. Add 2 onions, sliced. Cut 6 to 8 stalks of celery into 6-inch pieces, and arrange on top of the onions like a rack to hold the chicken breast halves. Put the chicken on the celery, and sprinkle with garlic, salt and pepper. Cover tightly with foil, and bake at 350 degrees for 40 minutes. The chicken will be delicious and after discarding the mushy vegetables, there will be a wonderful broth for soups and sauces.

2 **cups cubed, cooked chicken breast**	½ **cup diagonally sliced snow peas**
2 **cups seedless grapes**	3 **tablespoons slivered almonds, toasted**
1 **cup thinly sliced red bell pepper**	2 **tablespoons chopped green onion**
1 **cup thinly sliced yellow bell pepper**	**Creamy Herb Dressing**

Combine chicken, grapes, bell peppers, snow peas, almonds and onion in a serving bowl. Toss with dressing to coat.

Yield: 6 main-dish servings

Creamy Herb Dressing:

¼ **cup low-fat yogurt**	½ **teaspoon dried tarragon**
¼ **cup low-fat mayonnaise**	½ **teaspoon dried thyme**
1 **teaspoon salt**	⅛ **teaspoon pepper**
½ **teaspoon Dijon mustard**	⅛ **teaspoon dried rosemary**

Combine ingredients in a small bowl, stirring until well blended. Cover and refrigerate until ready to serve.

Yield: ½ cup

Korean Salad

1 (10-ounce) bag fresh spinach, torn into pieces
1 cup bean sprouts
¼ pound bacon, cooked and crumbled
1 (8-ounce) can sliced water chestnuts, drained
4 hard-cooked eggs, chopped
1 cup vegetable oil
¾ cups sugar
⅓ cup ketchup
¼ cup vinegar
2 teaspoons salt
1 teaspoon Worcestershire sauce
1 small onion, chopped

Combine spinach, bean sprouts, bacon, water chestnuts and eggs in a serving bowl. Combine oil, sugar, ketchup, vinegar, salt, Worcestershire and onion in a small bowl, whisking until well blended. Pour over salad, tossing to coat.

Yield: 8 to 10 servings

Mexican Salad

1 (10-ounce) package frozen corn, thawed
2 cups sliced zucchini
1 (7-ounce) jar roasted red bell peppers, drained and cut into strips
¾ cup olive oil
¼ cup apple cider vinegar
2 teaspoons salt
1 teaspoon sugar
1 teaspoon curry powder
1 clove garlic, pressed

Cook corn according to package directions; drain. Combine corn, zucchini and bell peppers in a bowl. Combine oil, vinegar, salt, sugar, curry and garlic in a small bowl; pour over vegetables, tossing to coat. Let stand at room temperature 1 hour to blend flavors. Cover and refrigerate until well chilled. Drain vegetables, reserving dressing. Serve vegetables over lettuce with dressing on the side.

Yield: 6 servings

Deli Fix-Up

1	pint chicken salad
2	tablespoons shredded cheddar or Swiss cheese

Seasoned croutons

Place salad in an ungreased 2-cup baking dish. Sprinkle with cheese and top with croutons. Bake at 300 degrees for 20 minutes or until thoroughly heated.

Yield: 2 servings

Mushroom and Pepper Salad

1 green bell pepper
1 red bell pepper
¾ cup celery, diagonally sliced
6 tablespoons olive oil, divided
2 cups sliced fresh mushrooms

4 teaspoons red wine vinegar
4 teaspoons lemon juice
½ teaspoon sugar
2 Belgian endive
¼ cup sliced green onions

Cut green and red pepper into 1 ½ x ½-inch pieces. Cook peppers and celery strips in boiling water for 45 seconds; remove with a slotted spoon and immediately place in ice water to cool. Drain and place vegetables in a mixing bowl. Heat 2 tablespoons olive oil in a large skillet over medium-high heat; add mushrooms and sauté until tender; drain excess liquid. Add to vegetables; cover and refrigerate until well chilled. Combine ¼ cup oil, vinegar, lemon juice and sugar in a small bowl. Cover and refrigerate until chilled. Combine vegetables and dressing, tossing to coat. Separate endive leaves and arrange on a serving platter. Fill endive leaves with vegetable mixture. Sprinkle with green onions.

Yield: 6 to 8 servings

SOUPS, SALADS, & SANDWICHES

Overnight Coleslaw

1	medium head cabbage, shredded (about 12 cups)	1	cup vinegar
2	carrots, peeled and grated	¾	cup vegetable oil
1	red onion, chopped	1	teaspoon dry mustard
1	green bell pepper, chopped	1	teaspoon celery seed
1	cup plus 2 teaspoons sugar, divided	1	teaspoon salt

Combine cabbage, carrots, onion and pepper in a large bowl; sprinkle with 1 cup sugar and set aside. Combine remaining 2 teaspoons sugar, vinegar, oil, dry mustard, celery seed and salt in a saucepan over medium-high heat; bring mixture to a boil. Remove from heat and pour dressing over cabbage mixture, stirring to coat. Cover and refrigerate 8 hours or overnight. Stir well before serving.

Yield: 12 to 16 servings

Pickled Mushrooms

1	cup red wine vinegar	2	whole cloves
½	cup cold water	½	bay leaf
2	teaspoons salt	1	pound small, white mushrooms (if large, halve or quarter)
5	whole black peppercorns		
2	cloves garlic, peeled and crushed	1	tablespoon vegetable oil

Combine vinegar, water, salt, peppercorns, garlic, cloves and bay leaf in a 2-quart enameled or stainless steel saucepan over high heat. Bring to a boil, stir in mushrooms and reduce heat to low. Simmer, uncovered, for 10 minutes, stirring occasionally. Let cool to room temperature. Remove garlic from marinade and pour the entire contents of the pan into a 1-quart jar. Slowly pour oil on top; secure the top with plastic and cover tightly. Marinate the mushrooms in the refrigerator for at least 1 week.

Yield: 6 to 8 servings

SOUPS, SALADS, & SANDWICHES

🌿 Garden Potato Salad

*Bring out your old wooden salad bowl and fill with lettuce
and greens and decorate with freshly picked nasturtium blossoms.*

4	medium potatoes	1	(10-ounce) package frozen peas, thawed
⅔	cup apple cider vinegar		
⅓	cup vegetable oil	12	cherry tomatoes, halved
½	teaspoon salt		Garnish: lettuce leaves, fresh parsley
¼	teaspoon pepper		

Cook potatoes in boiling water to cover 30 minutes or until tender. Drain and cool slightly. Peel, slice and place in a large serving bowl. Combine vinegar, oil, salt and pepper; pour over warm potatoes, tossing lightly. Gently stir in peas and tomatoes. Cover and refrigerate 8 hours or overnight. Garnish with lettuce leaves and parsley.

Yield: 8 servings

Spicy Shrimp Salad

½	cup plus 1 tablespoon vegetable oil	½	cup minced celery
		2	tablespoon grated onion
3	tablespoons vinegar	2	tablespoons minced green bell pepper
2	tablespoons paprika		
2	tablespoons prepared mustard	2	tablespoons minced parsley
		1	pound peeled and cooked shrimp
1	teaspoon salt		
¼	teaspoon hot pepper sauce		Lettuce
1	hard-cooked egg, chopped		

Combine oil, vinegar, paprika, mustard, salt and pepper sauce in a large bowl, whisking until well blended. Stir in egg, celery, onion, bell pepper, parsley and shrimp. Cover and refrigerate before serving. Serve on a bed of lettuce or other greens.

Yield: 6 servings

Shoe String Chicken Salad

2	cups diced, cooked chicken	2	tablespoons onion, very finely chopped
2	cups chopped celery		Mayonnaise
¼	cup chopped green pepper		Salt
1	(8-ounce) package medium or sharp cheddar cheese, cubed	1	(2-ounce) can shoe string potatoes
6	hard-cooked eggs, chopped		
¼	cup pimiento-stuffed olives, sliced		

Combine chicken, celery, green pepper, cheese, eggs, olives and onion in a bowl; stir in just enough mayonnaise to hold mixture together. Season to taste with salt. Just before serving, stir in shoe string potatoes, adding more mayonnaise, if necessary. (The potatoes will lose their crunch if added too long before serving.)

Yield: 12 servings

Shrimp Salad

1	cup mayonnaise	2	tablespoons crab boil seasoning
½	cup crushed pineapple, drained	½	teaspoon dried dill weed
2	tablespoons chopped pimiento	2	pounds cooked and peeled shrimp, cut into large pieces

Combine mayonnaise, pineapple, pimiento, seasoning and dill in a large bowl, stirring to blend. Stir in shrimp. Cover and refrigerate until well chilled.

Yield: 6 to 8 servings

 Spinach-Apple Toss

Wash and place greens in a mesh laundry bag.
Run through spin cycle of washing machine.

8   ounces fresh spinach, torn
1   tart red apple, chopped
½   cup cooked and crumbled
    bacon

½   cup mayonnaise
¼   cup frozen orange juice
    concentrate, thawed

Toss spinach, apple and bacon in a serving bowl. Combine mayonnaise and juice concentrate and drizzle over salad.

Yield: 8 servings

Shrimp 'N Avocado Salad

1   pound cooked and peeled
    shrimp
1   (8-ounce) package
    mushrooms, sliced
1   cup thinly sliced celery
2   chopped tomatoes
1   large avocado, chopped
    Crisp salad greens, torn

½   cup wine or apple cider vinegar
5   tablespoons sugar or
    2 tablespoons honey
1   tablespoon soy sauce
1   teaspoon ground ginger
½   teaspoon dry or Dijon mustard
    Garlic powder
    Pepper

Combine shrimp, mushrooms, celery, tomatoes, avocado and greens in a large bowl. Combine vinegar, sugar, soy sauce, ginger and mustard in a jar; cover tightly and shake. Season to taste with garlic powder and pepper. Pour over salad, tossing to coat.

Yield: 4 servings

Tabbouleh

1 cup bulgur wheat	2 tomatoes, diced
1 cup boiling water	½ chopped fresh parsley
¼ cup lemon juice	½ cup chopped green bell pepper
1 ½ teaspoons salt	½ cup grated carrot
1 teaspoon minced garlic	3-4 ounces crumbled feta cheese
¼ cup olive oil	2 tablespoons fresh dill weed or
½ cup chopped green onions	2 teaspoons dried

Combine bulgur and boiling water in a large bowl; let stand ½ hour. Fluff with fork. Stir in ingredients in the order listed: lemon juice, salt, garlic, oil, green onions, tomatoes, parsley, bell pepper, carrot, cheese and dill. Cover and refrigerate at least 3 hours before serving.

Yield: 6 to 8 servings

Pasta Salad

A summer accompaniment to grilled fish or steak.

1 (16-ounce) package rotini pasta	1 teaspoon salt
1 cup vegetable oil	Raw vegetables such as broccoli florets, cauliflower
½ cup white wine vinegar	florets, sliced zucchini,
½ cup sugar	sliced green or red onion,
1 tablespoon dried Italian seasoning or dill weed	sliced green or red bell pepper, sliced ripe or
2 teaspoon dry mustard	pimiento-stuffed olives

Cook rotini according to package directions; drain. Rinse in cold water; drain. Combine oil, vinegar, sugar, Italian seasoning, dry mustard and salt in a bowl, whisking until well blended. Combine pasta, dressing and vegetables in a large serving bowl, tossing to coat. Cover and refrigerate until well chilled. Toss gently before serving.

Yield: 8 to 10 servings

🍃 *Strawberry-Spinach Salad* ✓

*Strawberries will stay firm for several days
if you put them in the refrigerator in a colander.
Don't wash strawberries until they are ready for use.*

1 (10-ounce) package fresh spinach, torn	1 cup celery, cut diagonally
1 pint strawberries, halved	Glazed Pecans
	Poppy Seed Dressing

Combine spinach, strawberries and celery in a large salad bowl. Sprinkle with pecans, toss lightly. Toss salad with enough dressing to coat, just before serving or serve dressing on the side.

Yield: 8 to 10 servings

Glazed Pecans:

⅔ cup sugar	1 cup pecan halves

Heat sugar in a heavy skillet over medium-high heat, stirring until melted. Add pecans, stirring to coat. Turn pecans out onto lightly greased aluminum foil; let cool. Recipe may be prepared ahead. Store pecans in an airtight container.

Yield: 1 cup

Poppy Seed Dressing:

⅔ cup apple cider vinegar	½ teaspoon salt
½ cup sugar	2 teaspoons dry mustard
4 green onions, sliced	2 cups vegetable oil
3 tablespoons poppy seeds	

Combine vinegar, sugar, onion, poppy seeds, salt and dry mustard in a blender; process until mixed well. With blender running, gradually add oil in a slow steady stream.

Yield: 3 cups

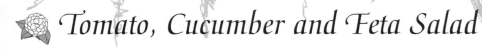Tomato, Cucumber and Feta Salad

1	pound cucumbers	1	tablespoon finely chopped fresh thyme
3	tomatoes, quartered		
4	green onions, finely sliced	2	tablespoons extra-virgin olive oil
1	(8-ounce) package feta cheese, cut into small cubes		
		2	tablespoons white wine vinegar
2	tablespoons finely chopped fresh mint		Salt
1	tablespoon finely chopped fresh chives		Freshly ground pepper

Cut cucumbers in quarters lengthwise and cut into ¼-inch slices. Combine cucumbers, tomatoes, green onions, feta, mint, chives and thyme in a large salad bowl. Whisk together oil, vinegar, salt and pepper; pour over salad, tossing to coat. Serve chilled.

Yield: 4 to 6 servings

Grecian Tossed Salad

½	head iceberg lettuce, torn	¼	cup chopped green bell pepper
4-5	endive leaves, torn	½	cup feta cheese, crumbled
4	radishes, sliced	6	ripe olives, sliced
3	green onions, chopped	¼	cup olive oil
1	tomato, cut into wedges	2	tablespoons vinegar
½	cucumber, thinly sliced	1	teaspoon whole oregano

Combine lettuce, endive, radish, onion, tomato, cucumber, bell pepper, cheese and olives in a large bowl. Combine oil, vinegar and oregano in jar; screw lid tightly, and shake well. Toss with salad just before serving.

Yield: 8 servings

Pasta Chicken Salad

1 (16-ounce) package spinach rotini, cooked and drained
1 (10-ounce) package frozen peas, thawed
2 cups cubed, cooked chicken
1 cup chopped celery
⅓ cup chopped onion

1 cup mayonnaise
1 cup milk
1 (1-ounce) envelope buttermilk salad dressing mix
3 tablespoons minced fresh dill weed or 1 tablespoon dried
½ teaspoon garlic salt

Combine pasta, peas, chicken, celery and onion in a large bowl, mixing well. Combine mayonnaise, milk, dressing mix, dill weed and garlic salt in a small bowl, whisking until smooth. Pour dressing over salad, tossing to coat. Cover and refrigerate for at least 2 to 3 hours before serving.

Yield: 10 to 12 servings

Crab-Egg Salad Magnifique

1 (8-ounce) package cream cheese, softened
3 tablespoons mayonnaise
1 ½ teaspoons cream-style prepared horseradish
1 (6-ounce) package frozen crabmeat, thawed and drained

6 hard-cooked eggs, chopped
½ cup chopped celery
½ cup chopped red or green bell pepper
6 croissants, split
Lettuce

Combine cream cheese, mayonnaise and horseradish in a medium bowl, mixing well. Add crabmeat, eggs, celery and bell pepper, mixing lightly. Cover and refrigerate until well chilled. Serve on croissants with lettuce.

Yield: 6 servings

SOUPS, SALADS, & SANDWICHES

 Tortilla Rollups

2	(8-ounce) packages cream cheese, softened	½	cup diced red and yellow bell peppers
1	(1-ounce) envelope buttermilk salad dressing mix	½	cup diced celery
2	green onions, sliced	1	(2.24-ounce) can sliced ripe olives, drained
4	large flour tortillas	1	(4 ½-ounce) can diced green chiles, drained

Combine cream cheese, dressing mix and green onions in a small bowl; spread over 1 side of tortillas. Sprinkle bell peppers, celery, olives and chiles over cream cheese; roll up tortillas. Cover with plastic wrap and refrigerate until well chilled. Cut into ½-inch slices.

Yield: 16 servings

Stuffed Italian Loaf

1	loaf Italian bread	½	cup shredded cheddar cheese
¼	cup mayonnaise	2	tablespoons chopped onion
⅓	cup chopped fresh parsley	¼	teaspoon salt
1	(8-ounce) package cream cheese, softened		Dill pickle slices
¾	cup chopped celery		Deli ham or other cold cuts

Cut bread lengthwise and hollow out middle. Place bread shells, top side down, on a working surface. Spread mayonnaise on both sides and sprinkle with parsley. Combine cream cheese, celery, cheddar, onion and salt. Spread on both sides of bread. Roll pickle in cold cuts and place in bottom half of bread; cover with top half. Wrap tightly with plastic wrap and secure with a rubber band. Refrigerate several hours or overnight until well chilled. Cut slices ½ to ¾ inches thick and serve.

Yield: 10 to 12 servings

Shrimp Sandwiches ✓

1	(3-ounce) package cream cheese, softened	8	ounces cooked and peeled shrimp, coarsely chopped
2	tablespoons mayonnaise	¼	cup finely chopped celery
1	tablespoon ketchup	¼	cup finely chopped green onions
1	teaspoon prepared mustard Dash garlic powder	10	slices sandwich bread, lightly buttered

Combine cream cheese and mayonnaise in a medium bowl; stir in ketchup, mustard and garlic powder. Add shrimp, celery and green onions, stirring to blend. Place shrimp mixture between slices of buttered bread to make 5 whole sandwiches. Cut each in half or quarters.

Yield: 10 halves or 20 tea sandwiches

Tunaburgers

1	(7-ounce) can tuna, drained	⅓	cup mayonnaise
½	cup chopped celery	2	tablespoons chili sauce
½	cup fine, fresh bread crumbs (about 2 slices bread)	4	hamburger buns, toasted Lettuce
2	tablespoons minced onion		Tomato slices

Combine tuna, celery, bread crumbs and onion in a small bowl. Combine mayonnaise and chili sauce; stir into tuna mixture. Form mixture into 4 patties. Cook tunaburgers on a lightly oiled skillet over medium heat 5 minutes each side or until browned. Serve on buns with lettuce and tomatoes.

Yield: 4 servings

Turka-Rome Sandwiches

½	cup mayonnaise	12	slices Swiss cheese
1	tablespoon chopped dill pickle	6	slices salami
		6	slices tomato
1	teaspoon minced onion	6	slices turkey
12	slices Vienna bread	1	cup Italian salad dressing

Combine mayonnaise, pickle and onion in a small bowl. Spread mayonnaise mixture on 1 side of bread slices. Top 6 bread slices with 1 slice cheese, 1 slice each of cheese, salami, tomato, turkey and cheese. Cover with remaining bread slices, spread side down. Brush each side of sandwich with dressing. Grill or broil until golden brown.

Yield: 6 servings

Hearthside Sandwiches

2	cups finely chopped ham	2	tablespoons pickle relish, drained
1	cup (4 ounces) shredded sharp cheddar cheese	1	tablespoon grated onion
2	tablespoons mayonnaise	2	teaspoons prepared mustard
		8	sandwich buns

Combine ham, cheese, mayonnaise, relish, onion and mustard in a bowl. Spoon mixture into buns and wrap each sandwich in aluminum foil. Bake at 350 degrees for 20 minutes.

Yield: 8 servings

Pizza Burgers

A favorite with teens.

1	pound cooked ground beef	¼	cup pimiento-stuffed olives,
1	(6-ounce) can tomato sauce		sliced
1	cup (4 ounces) shredded	½	teaspoon salt
	cheese	¼	teaspoon garlic salt
			Sandwich buns

Combine beef, sauce, cheese, olives, salt and garlic salt in a bowl. Spoon mixture into buns and wrap each sandwich in aluminum foil. Refrigerate or freeze. Bake at 350 degrees for 20 minutes.

Yield: 6 to 8 servings

 # Barbequed Ham Sandwiches

¾	cup chili sauce	½	teaspoon paprika
3	tablespoons vinegar	½	teaspoon dry mustard
2	tablespoons brown sugar	1	pound shredded ham
2	tablespoons grape or currant		Sandwich buns
	jelly		

Combine chili sauce, vinegar, brown sugar, jelly, paprika and dry mustard in a saucepan over medium-high heat. Bring to a boil, reduce heat, and simmer 10 minutes. Stir in ham. Spoon mixture into buns. Recipe may be made ahead and reheated.

Yield: 6 to 8 servings

Enticing Entrées

Now to the meat of our cookbook. Succulent entrées, to entice the palates of distinguished diners, are essential to lush Low Country meals and *Twice Treasured Recipes*.

Enticing Entrées are introduced with a scene of silhouetted Spanish Moss, and the sun reflected in gentle Low Country waters of the Pinckney Island Nature Preserve. The limb's a perfect foothold for the "epiphyte", or air plant. It's a relative of a Low Country symbol for hospitality, the pineapple, and not a true moss. The graceful rootless herb isn't a parasite, and won't kill trees. It grows on air, absorbing rain, sunlight and dust, with minerals naturally leached from trees. Only if it's thick enough to block light or becomes rain drenched and weighs down weak limbs, will it injure trees. Spanish Moss holds 10 times its dry weight in liquid. The Indians and settlers used Spanish Moss to dress and soothe wounds, and as diapers. It's said to be a natural source of estrogen, contains acetyl salicylic acid (aspirin) and has anti-bacterial properties. Animals and birds nest with it, including squirrels, chickadees, mockingbirds, owls and egrets. Spanish Moss is still used by visitors and residents of Hilton Head for crafts, packing material and indoor mulch. April thru July in the Low Country the perfumed fragrance of tiny Spanish Moss flowers is at its peak.

Enticing Entrées are as versatile as Spanish Moss and taste so much better. The entrées are the heart of an intimate meal for two, or the soul of a buffet for twenty, gratifying the desires of the most demanding epicures, who never live on air alone.

Enticing
Entrées

Enticing Entrées

🌺**Quick and Easy Recipes are designated with a camellia flower.**
🍃 **Memorable Menu Recipes are designated with a leaf.**

Scallops with Grand Marnier and Angel Hair Pasta

3	tablespoons butter, divided	8	ounces angel hair pasta
1	pound sea scallops (halved, if very large)	1	cup fat-free sour cream
	Salt	1 ½	teaspoons lemon juice
	Pepper	1	teaspoon grated orange rind
½	cup minced shallots		Salt
1 ½	cups fat-free chicken broth		Pepper
½	cup white wine		Crushed herb-seasoned stuffing mix
¼	cup orange juice		Freshly grated Parmesan cheese
¼	cup Grand Marnier		

Melt 1 ½ tablespoons butter in a large skillet over medium-high heat. Add scallops and sprinkle with salt and pepper. Sauté for 1 minute, stirring constantly. Cover the skillet and cook the scallops, stirring occasionally, for 2 minutes or until opaque and slightly firm. Remove scallops with a slotted spoon and place on a large plate. Cover and keep warm

Add the shallots to the skillet; cook, stirring constantly, for 1 minute. Stir in the broth, wine, juice and liqueur. Bring mixture to a boil; reduce heat, and simmer until mixture is reduced to two-thirds cup. Cook pasta according to package directions until al dente; drain and place in a serving bowl. Cover to keep warm. Stir sour cream into sauce mixture and simmer until mixture is lightly thickened. Increase heat to medium-high and whisk in remaining 1 ½ teaspoons butter, lemon juice and orange rind. Season to taste with salt and pepper. Pour any accumulated juices from the scallops into the sauce. Pour over pasta; sprinkle with crushed stuffing and cheese.

Yield: 4 servings

 Cinnamon Spaghetti—Add cinnamon to your spaghetti sauce for added zip.

Shrimp and Veggie Spaghetti

4	slices bacon		1	teaspoon dried oregano
1	cup chopped onion		¼	teaspoon pepper
4	carrots, peeled and cut diagonally		¼	teaspoon garlic salt
¼	teaspoon garlic powder		1	pound medium shrimp, peeled and deveined
2	(14 ½-ounce) cans whole tomatoes		1	(8-ounce) package mushrooms, sliced
1	(2 ¼-ounce) can sliced ripe olives, drained			Hot cooked vermicelli
1	teaspoon dried basil			Freshly grated Parmesan cheese

Cook bacon in a large skillet over medium-high heat until crisp. Remove bacon, reserving 1 tablespoon drippings in skillet; crumble and set aside. Heat drippings over medium-high heat. Add onion, carrots and garlic powder and sauté until carrots are crisp-tender. Chop, but do not drain canned tomatoes. Stir tomatoes into carrot mixture. Add olives, basil, oregano, pepper and garlic salt. Bring mixture to a boil; reduce heat, and simmer for 3 to 5 minutes. Stir in shrimp and mushrooms; cook 10 minutes. Serve over cooked pasta; sprinkle with reserved bacon and Parmesan cheese.

Yield: 6 servings

Sweet and Sour Shrimp ✓

1 pound shrimp, cooked, peeled and deveined	¼ cup sugar
	2 tablespoons cornstarch
¼ cup margarine or vegetable oil	1 tablespoon soy sauce
	1 teaspoon ground ginger
1 onion, thinly sliced	½ teaspoon dry mustard
1 green bell pepper, cut into 1-inch squares	¼ teaspoon salt
	⅔ cup cherry tomatoes, halved or cut into wedges
2 (8 ¼-ounce) cans pineapple chunks in syrup, undrained	3 cups hot cooked rice
½ cup vinegar	½ cup slivered almonds, toasted

Melt margarine in a large skillet over medium-high heat. Add onion and bell pepper; sauté until tender, but not brown. Drain pineapple, reserving syrup. Combine pineapple syrup, vinegar, sugar, cornstarch, soy sauce, ginger, dry mustard and salt. Stir into vegetables. Bring mixture to a boil; boil 1 minute until thick and clear. Gently stir in pineapple chunks and tomatoes. Cut any large pieces of shrimp in half; stir shrimp into mixture. Cook until thoroughly heated. Combine rice and almonds and place on a serving platter. Spoon shrimp mixture over rice and serve.

Yield: 6 servings

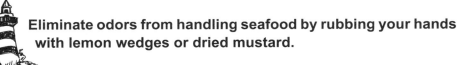

Eliminate odors from handling seafood by rubbing your hands with lemon wedges or dried mustard.

Shrimp Salad Bake

1 cup mayonnaise	2 ½ cups cooked, peeled and diced shrimp
1 teaspoon grated lemon peel	1 cup chopped celery
1 tablespoon fresh lemon juice	1 cup sliced almonds, toasted
1 tablespoon finely chopped onion	¾ cup (6 ounces) shredded sharp cheddar cheese, divided
1 teaspoon dry vermouth	1 ½ tablespoons butter, melted
½ teaspoon salt	1 cup cracker crumbs
Dash hot pepper sauce	

Combine mayonnaise, peel, juice, onion, vermouth, salt and pepper sauce in a large bowl. Stir in shrimp, celery, almonds and ½ cup cheese. Spoon mixture into 8, individual baking shells or a lightly greased 11 x 7 x 1 ½-inch baking dish. Combine butter and crumbs; stir in remaining ¼ cup cheese. Sprinkle evenly over shrimp mixture. Bake at 400 degrees for 20 to 30 minutes until thoroughly heated.

Yield: 8 servings

Low-Fat Shrimp Curry

2 tablespoons diet margarine	1 tablespoon skim milk
1 stalk celery, finely chopped	½ cup low-fat cottage cheese
¼ small onion, finely chopped	¾ pound boiled shrimp, peeled and deveined
¼ apple, finely chopped	Pepper
¼ cup water	
1 ½ teaspoons curry powder	

Melt margarine in a large skillet over medium-high heat. Add celery, onion and apple; sauté until tender. Add water and curry powder; cook until most of the liquid evaporates. Meanwhile, combine milk and cottage cheese in a blender; process until smooth. Stir cheese mixture into curry mixture. Stir in shrimp. Season to taste with pepper. Serve over rice.

Yield: 4 servings

Three Star Seafood Luncheon Dish ✓

This recipe can be made ahead and refrigerated. Remove and bring to room temperature before baking. All shrimp may be used, if desired.

1 **(10 ¾-ounce) can cream of shrimp soup**	½ **pound crabmeat or lobster**
½ **can milk**	1 **(5 ½-ounce) can sliced water chestnuts, drained**
½ **cup mayonnaise**	2 **cups uncooked very fine**
¼ **(1 ounce) shredded cheddar cheese**	**noodles (do not crush)**
½ **pound (small to medium) peeled and deveined shrimp**	1 **(3 ½-ounce) can French fried onion rings, crushed**

Combine soup, milk, mayonnaise and cheese in a large bowl. Stir in shrimp, crabmeat, water chestnuts and noodles. Pour mixture into a greased 2-quart baking dish. Bake, covered, at 350 degrees for 20 minutes. Uncover and bake 10 minutes. Sprinkle with crushed onion rings and bake 10 minutes or until noodles are tender.

Yield: 6 servings

Herbed Shrimp and Feta Casserole

2	large eggs	4	cloves garlic, minced
1	cup evaporated milk	½	pound angel hair pasta, cooked
1	cup plain yogurt		
1	(8-ounce) package crumbled feta cheese	1	(16-ounce) jar mild, chunky salsa
1 ¼	(5 ounces) cups shredded Swiss cheese	1	pound uncooked medium shrimp, peeled
⅓	cup chopped fresh parsley	2	cups (8 ounces) shredded mozzarella cheese
1	teaspoon dried basil		
1	teaspoon dried oregano		

Combine eggs, milk, yogurt, feta and Swiss cheese, parsley, basil, oregano and garlic in a small bowl. Spread half of pasta over bottom of an 11 x 7 x 1 ½-inch baking dish coated with cooking spray. Cover with salsa; add half of shrimp. Spread remaining pasta over shrimp. Spread egg mixture over pasta. Top with remaining shrimp and sprinkle with mozzarella cheese. Bake at 350 degrees for 30 minutes. Remove from oven and let stand 10 minutes before serving.

Yield: 10 servings

Baked Salmon for 4 or More

2	large filets of salmon	⅔	cup ketchup
	Sliced onion	⅓	cup maple syrup
	Sliced lemons		Garlic powder or minced garlic
6-8	slices bacon, cooked and crumbled		Salt
			Pepper

Place salmon in a large baking pan. Place onion slices, lemon slices and bacon over salmon. Combine ketchup, syrup, garlic powder, salt and pepper in a small bowl; pour over salmon. Bake, covered, at 350 degrees for 45 minutes.

Yield: 4 servings

Barbecued Shrimp

"The fastest way to clean 'a mess a shrimp'
is to let each person clean his own."

1 ½ cups butter
1 (8-ounce) bottle Italian salad
    dressing
⅓ cup lemon juice
¼ cup olive oil

2-3 tablespoons ground black
    pepper
1 tablespoon Worcestershire
    sauce
½ teaspoon hot pepper sauce
5 pounds unpeeled shrimp

Melt butter in a large roasting pan. Stir in salad dressing, lemon juice, oil, pepper, Worcestershire and hot pepper sauce. Add shrimp, mixing well. Bake, covered, at 350 degrees for 35 minutes, stirring occasionally, or until shrimp turn bright pink. Serve the shrimp and sauce in soup bowls with plenty of crusty bread along with a tossed salad.

Yield: 8 to 10 servings

Hilton Head Crab Casserole ✓

8 slices bread
2 ½ cups crabmeat
2 stalks celery, diced
1 small onion, diced
1 small green bell pepper, diced

½ cup mayonnaise
4 large eggs
3 cups milk
1 cup (4 ounces) grated sharp
    cheddar cheese

Trim crusts from bread and slice into 1-inch cubes. Place half of bread into a buttered 11 x 7 x 1 ½-inch baking dish. Combine crabmeat, celery, onion, bell pepper and mayonnaise in a bowl; spread over bread. Top with remaining bread cubes. Beat together eggs and milk; pour over crabmeat mixture. Cover and refrigerate 8 hours or overnight. Uncover and sprinkle with cheese. Bake at 350 degrees for 1 hour 15 minutes. Cut into squares.

Salmon Salad Pie

1 (10-ounce) package frozen chopped broccoli, thawed
1 (9-inch) unbaked pie shell
1 cup mayonnaise
1 cup (4 ounces) shredded Swiss cheese

1 (7 ¾-ounce) can salmon, drained and flaked
⅓ cup diced celery
¼ cup sliced green onion
3 hard-cooked eggs, chopped
½ teaspoons dill weed
⅛ teaspoon pepper

Cook broccoli according to package directions; drain. Arrange broccoli in the bottom of pie shell; set aside. Combine mayonnaise, cheese, salmon, celery, onion, eggs, dill and pepper in a bowl; spoon over broccoli. Bake at 375 degrees for 30 minutes. Serve warm or chilled.

Yield: 6 servings

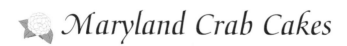# Maryland Crab Cakes

1 pound lump crabmeat, picked and flaked
1 large egg, lightly beaten
2-3 tablespoons prepared mustard
2 tablespoons mayonnaise

1 tablespoon chopped fresh parsley
½ teaspoon Old Bay seasoning
6 saltines, crushed
2 tablespoons shortening

Combine crab, egg, mustard, mayonnaise, parsley, seasoning and crushed crackers in a large bowl, mixing gently. Shape into 8 to 10 crab cakes. Melt 2 tablespoons shortening in a large skillet over medium-high heat. Add crab cakes and fry on both sides until golden brown.

Yield: 8 to 10 cakes

Crabmeat Casserole with Artichoke Hearts ✓

2 tablespoons butter	1 pound fresh crabmeat, cleaned
1 (8-ounce) package mushrooms, sliced	White Sauce
	¼ cup grated Parmesan cheese
1 (14½-ounce) can artichoke hearts, drained	

Melt butter in a large skillet over medium-high heat. Add mushrooms and sauté until tender; drain. Place artichoke hearts in the bottom of a lightly greased shallow casserole dish; cover with crabmeat. Add sautéed mushrooms. Pour White Sauce over mushrooms and sprinkle with cheese. Bake at 375 degrees for 20 minutes.

Yield: 4 servings

White Sauce:

2 tablespoons butter	1 tablespoon Worcestershire sauce
2½ tablespoons all-purpose flour	Salt
1 cup heavy whipping cream	Cayenne pepper
½ cup medium dry sherry	

Melt butter in a heavy saucepan over medium heat; add flour, whisking until smooth. Cook 1 minute, whisking constantly. Gradually add cream, sherry and Worcestershire; cook, whisking constantly, until mixture is thickened and bubbly. Season to taste with salt and cayenne pepper.

Yield: 1¾ cups

---

*Cooking is like love.
It should be entered into
with abandon or not at all.*

Baked Fish Fillets

2	pounds fish steaks or fillets	2	tablespoons Parmesan cheese
1	cup sour cream		
2	tablespoons dry onion soup mix	1	tablespoons chopped fresh parsley
2	teaspoons lemon juice	¼	teaspoon paprika
1	cup fine, dry bread crumbs	¼	cup butter, melted

Cut fish into 6 portions; pat dry with paper towels. Set aside. Combine sour cream, soup mix and lemon juice in a small bowl; set aside. Combine bread crumbs, cheese, parsley and paprika in a shallow dish. Coat fish in sour cream mixture and dredge in crumb mixture. Place in a lightly greased, shallow baking pan. Drizzle with butter. Bake at 500 degrees for 10 to 12 minutes or until fish flakes easily with a fork.

Yield: 6 servings

Chicken Livers Stroganoff

1	tablespoon vegetable oil	2	tablespoons ketchup
1	onion, chopped	¼	teaspoon salt
2	cups (6 ounces) sliced mushrooms	⅛	teaspoon pepper
8	ounces chicken livers	½	cup sour cream or plain yogurt
1	tablespoon all-purpose flour	1	tablespoon chopped fresh dill weed or 1 teaspoon dried
¼	cup white wine		
2	tablespoons chicken broth	¼	teaspoon mace

Heat oil in a large skillet over medium-high heat. Add onion and sauté 5 minutes until golden brown. Add mushrooms and sauté 3 to 4 minutes, adding more oil, if necessary. Add chicken livers; sauté 6 to 8 minutes. Stir in flour, whisking until smooth. Cook 1 minute, stirring constantly. Stir in wine, broth, ketchup, salt and pepper. Cover and simmer for 10 minutes. Stir in sour cream, dill and mace. Cook until thoroughly heated and serve over brown rice.

Yield: 2 servings

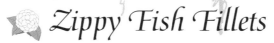 Zippy Fish Fillets

Cook fish only until it flakes easily when tested with a fork.
Overcooking spoils the flavor and toughens the texture of fish.

2	pounds fish fillets, cut into serving pieces	1	teaspoon salt
¼	cup butter, melted	1	teaspoon grated onion
2	tablespoons lime juice	1	teaspoon paprika
			Dash pepper

Arrange fish in a lightly greased baking dish. Combine butter, juice, salt, onion, paprika and pepper in a small bowl; pour over fish. Bake at 350 degrees for 20 minutes.

Yield: 6 servings

Stan Smith's Quick Cranberry Chicken

When pounding chicken breasts between plastic wrap,
sprinkle with a little water. The meat will not tear.

12	boneless, skinless chicken breasts	1	(8-ounce) bottle Russian salad dressing
1	(14 ½-ounce) can whole-berry cranberry sauce	1	(1-ounce) envelope onion soup mix

Arrange chicken breasts in a large, lightly greased baking dish. Combine cranberry sauce, salad dressing and soup mix in a small bowl; pour over chicken. Bake at 350 degrees for approximately 1 hour. This recipe may be halved to serve 6.

Yield: 12 servings

Chicken Cheese Lasagna

½ cup butter	1 teaspoon dried oregano
1 onion, chopped	½ teaspoon white pepper
1 clove garlic, minced	2 cups ricotta cheese
½ cup all-purpose flour	1 tablespoon minced fresh parsley
1 teaspoon salt	
2 cups chicken broth	8 ounces lasagna noodles, cooked
1½ cups milk	
4 cups (1 pound) shredded mozzarella cheese, divided	2 (10-ounce) packages frozen chopped spinach, thawed and drained
1 cup grated Parmesan, divided	
1 teaspoon dried basil	2 cups cubed, cooked chicken

Melt butter in a saucepan over medium heat. Add onion and garlic; sauté until tender. Stir in flour and salt, whisking until smooth. Cook 1 minute, whisking constantly. Gradually add broth and milk; cook over medium heat, whisking constantly, until mixture is thickened and bubbly. Stir in 2 cups mozzarella, ½ cup Parmesan cheese, basil, oregano and pepper; set aside. Combine ricotta, parsley and remaining 2 cups mozzarella; set aside. Spread ¼ of the cheese sauce into a greased 13 x 9 x 2-inch baking dish; cover with one-third of the noodles. Top noodles with one-half of the ricotta mixture, one-half of the spinach and one-half of the chicken. Cover with one-forth of the cheese sauce and one-third of the noodles. Repeat layers of ricotta mixture, spinach, chicken and one-fourth cheese sauce. Cover with remaining noodles and cheese sauce. Sprinkle remaining ½ cup Parmesan cheese over all. Bake at 350 degrees, uncovered for 35 to 40 minutes. Let stand for 15 minutes before serving.

Yield: 12 servings

Chicken Carlotta

1	tablespoon olive oil	1	cup dry white wine
4	boneless, skinless chicken breast halves	½	cup diced tomatoes
		¼	cup chopped green onions
1	(8-ounce) package mushrooms, sliced	3	tablespoons fresh lemon juice
		1	teaspoon dried dill weed
1	(14-ounce) can artichoke hearts, drained and halved	¼	teaspoon ground cinnamon
		⅛	teaspoon nutmeg
3	cloves garlic, minced		Hot cooked brown rice
2	tablespoons capers, drained	⅓	cup crumbled feta cheese

Heat oil in a large skillet over medium-high heat. Add chicken and sauté until lightly browned; remove and keep warm. Add mushrooms, artichoke hearts, garlic and capers to skillet, stirring to mix well. Stir in wine. Add tomatoes, green onion, juice, dill, cinnamon and nutmeg. Cook, stirring constantly, until sauce thickens. Add chicken; cook until mixture is thoroughly heated and chicken is done. Serve over brown rice and sprinkle with feta cheese.

Yield: 4 servings

Baked Garlic with a Little Chicken

*Submerge chicken breasts in buttermilk 3 to 4 hours in
the refrigerator before cooking for moist and tender chicken.*

6	boneless, skinless chicken breasts	3	sprigs fresh thyme
	Lemon juice	1	sprig fresh rosemary
2	stalks celery with leaves, chopped	1	sprig fresh dill weed
			Kosher salt
1	fennel bulb, chopped		Freshly ground pepper
¼	cup olive oil	1	head elephant garlic (entire bulb)
¼	cup white wine		

Place chicken in a large baking dish; sprinkle with lemon juice, tossing to coat breasts. Combine celery, fennel, oil, wine, thyme, rosemary, dill, salt and pepper; spread over chicken. Separate cloves of garlic and arrange them in the corners of the dish. Cover tightly with foil. Bake at 325 degrees for 2 hours. Serve with lightly toasted French bread. Encourage guests to squeeze the garlic out of the skin and spread it on the bread. A spicy salad goes well with this dish. The recipe invites you to use your imagination with seasonings. Fennel seeds and a few drops of hot sauce, or more lemon juice may be added. This is a fun dish to work with.

Yield: 6 servings

Parsley and Parmesan Baked Chicken

¼ cup Italian salad dressing	½ cup grated Parmesan cheese
¼ cup white wine	⅓ cup fine, dry bread crumbs
1 (3 to 3 ½-pound) chicken, cut up	2 tablespoons chopped fresh parsley
1 large egg, lightly beaten	½ teaspoon salt
1 tablespoon water	⅛ teaspoon pepper

Combine salad dressing and wine in a 13 x 9 x 2-inch baking dish; add chicken pieces, turning to coat all sides. Cover and refrigerate at least 4 hours, turn chicken occasionally. Drain chicken, reserving marinade. Combine egg and water in a small bowl. Combine cheese, bread crumbs, parsley, salt and pepper in a large plastic bag. Dip each chicken piece in egg mixture; drain. Add to crumb mixture, shaking to coat. Repeat with remaining ingredients. Return chicken to baking dish; spoon reserved marinade over top. Bake at 350 degrees for 45 to 50 minutes or until tender.

Yield: 4 servings

---

*Overheard while in line
at The Bargain Box:*

*The Bargain Box is the one place
I know where if you're a compulsive
shopper you can walk out happy
and have spent $10.00 or less!*

Chicken Casserole Supreme

Cook the chicken breasts (with skin and bones) and
add onion, bay leaf, celery and a chicken bouillon cube
to make good broth for the stuffing mix.

3 pounds bone-in chicken breasts, cooked and chopped	1 cup mayonnaise
1 (10¾-ounce) can cream of mushroom soup	2 cups (8 ounces) shredded cheddar cheese
1 (8-ounce) package mushrooms, sliced	½ cup butter or margarine, melted
1 cup sour cream	1½ cups chicken broth
	2 (6-ounce) packages cornbread stuffing mix

Combine chicken, soup, mushrooms, sour cream and mayonnaise in a large bowl. Spread into a greased 13 x 9 x 2-inch baking pan. Sprinkle with cheese. Combine butter, broth, cornbread mix and 1 of the enclosed seasoning packets; stir well. Spoon over cheese. Bake at 350 degrees for 35 to 40 minutes or until thoroughly heated.

Oven Fried Chicken Chimichangas

3   (5-ounce) cans white chicken, drained
1   (4-ounce) can chopped green chiles, drained
1   cup (4 ounces) shredded Monterey Jack cheese
½   cup sliced green onions

8   (9-inch) flour tortillas
Butter-flavored vegetable cooking spray
Shredded lettuce
Salsa
Sour cream

Combine chicken, chiles, cheese and onion in a medium bowl. Wrap tortillas in damp paper towels; microwave at HIGH for 15 seconds until hot. Coat both sides with vegetable cooking spray. Spoon ½ cup of chicken mixture in the center of a tortilla. Fold up sides, then bottom; roll to completely cover filling. Place rolls, seam side down, on a greased baking sheet. Bake at 425 degrees for 10 minutes or until golden brown. Serve with lettuce, salsa and sour cream on top.

Yield: 8 servings

A smiling face is half the meal.

Salsa Couscous Chicken

1	cup couscous or rice	¼	cup water
1	tablespoon olive oil	2	tablespoons dried currants or
¼	cup almonds, coarsely		raisins
	chopped	1	teaspoon honey
2	garlic cloves, minced	¾	teaspoon ground cumin
8	skinless chicken thighs	½	teaspoon ground cinnamon
1	cup chunky salsa		

Cook couscous or rice according to package directions; keep warm. Heat oil in a large skillet over medium-high heat. Add almonds and sauté 1 to 2 minutes until golden brown. Remove almonds; set aside. Add garlic to skillet; sauté for 30 seconds, stirring constantly. Add chicken; sauté 4 to 5 minutes or until brown on both sides. Combine salsa, water, currants, honey, cumin and cinnamon in a small bowl; add to chicken, mixing well. Bring mixture to a boil; reduce heat, and simmer for 20 minutes, stirring occasionally. Stir in almonds. Serve with hot couscous or rice.

Yield: 4 servings

Five Hour Chuck Roast Stew

1	(1 ½ to 2-pound) chuck roast	1	(16-ounce) package baby
	Garlic salt		carrots
	Pepper	1	(10 ¾-ounce) can tomato
8-12	small new potatoes, washed		soup
	and quartered	1	(10 ¾-ounce) can cream of
2	large Vidalia onions, chopped		chicken soup

Sprinkle chuck roast with garlic salt and pepper; place in a large roasting pan. Arrange potatoes, onions, and carrots around roast. Spoon soups over all ingredients; cover tightly with foil. Bake at 250 degrees for 5 hours. (Do not peek!)

Yield: 4 to 6 servings

Rock Cornish Game Hens with Raspberry Sauce

*When the occasion calls for a sophisticated entrée,
nothing fills the bill like a platter of baked Cornish hens.*

4	Cornish hens, split in half	8	lemon wedges
¼	cup butter, softened		Raspberry Sauce
	White pepper		

Rub hen halves with butter and sprinkle all sides lightly with white pepper. Place each hen in a shallow baking dish or roasting pan, cut side down, on a lemon wedge. Bake at 350 degrees; after 15 minutes baste with a small amount of raspberry sauce. Continue baking for 45 minutes, basting occasionally. (This dish may be refrigerated and reheated just before serving. Bake at 400 degrees for 15 to 20 minutes until thoroughly heated.) Serve with Raspberry Sauce.

Yield: 8 servings

Raspberry Sauce:

2	(10-ounce) packages frozen raspberries, thawed	¼	cup fresh lemon juice
¼	cup water	2	tablespoons cornstarch
		½	teaspoon ground ginger

Press raspberries through a fine sieve over a non-aluminum saucepan to remove seeds. Combine water, juice, cornstarch and ginger; stir into raspberries. Cook over medium heat, stirring constantly, until mixture boils. Boil 1 minute, stirring constantly. Remove from heat.

Yield: 2½ cups

Cornish hens are a cross between the Plymouth Rock chicken and the English Cornish gamecock. It's a tender breasted bird with little fat and maximum white meat. Pungently stuffed Cornish hens are a delicious main attraction to spark any dinner party.

Duck with Grape Sauce

*Pungently tasting ducks are a delicious
main attraction to any dinner party.*

2	(5-pound) ducks		Sliced onions
	Salt	2	cups white wine
	Pepper	2	tablespoons honey
	Lemon juice		Grape Sauce
	Celery leaves		

Trim the wing tips and cut off the neck of the ducks. Rinse inside and out with cold water; dry. Sprinkle with salt and pepper. Rub the inside cavities with lemon juice and add a few celery leaves and onion slices. Prick skin and place on a rack in a broiler pan. Bake at 325 degrees for 30 minutes. Drain fat from pan. Pour wine over ducks. Bake, basting frequently with pan juices, until ducks are tender (about 20 minutes per pound). Brush with honey and bake 15 minutes until golden brown. Pour off drippings, reserving 2 tablespoons for Grape Sauce. Place ducks on a serving platter; brush with a small amount of sauce. Pass remaining sauce.

Yield: 6 servings

Grape Sauce:

2	tablespoons reserved drippings	¾	cup fresh orange juice
3	tablespoons grated orange peel	¾	cup chicken broth
		¾	cup orange liqueur
		1 ½	cups seedless white grapes

Combine drippings, juice, broth and liqueur in a saucepan or roasting pan used to cook ducks. Bring mixture to a boil; reduce heat, and simmer until reduced to 1 ½ cups. Strain mixture and stir in peel and grapes.

Yield: about 2 ½ cups

Eye of Round Roast

¼	cup coarsely ground pepper	1	tablespoon ketchup or tomato paste
1	teaspoon ground cardamom	1	teaspoon paprika
1	(4 to 5-pound) eye of round steak		Dash garlic powder or 1 clove garlic, minced
⅔	cup soy sauce		
½	cup vinegar		

Combine pepper and cardamom on a large piece of wax paper. Roll beef, pressing spices into meat. Combine soy sauce, vinegar, ketchup, paprika and garlic powder in a large plastic bag. Add beef; seal and refrigerate 8 hours or overnight, turning occasionally. Remove beef from marinade, reserving marinade. Grill or bake according to procedures below:

To grill: Sear beef on a grill over hot coals; place on a large piece of foil. Wrap beef, including some or all of the marinade. Discard any remaining marinade. Grill until meat thermometer registers 140 degrees for rare, 160 degrees for medium or 170 for well done.

To bake: Bake at 300 degrees, covered for 1 ½ hours for medium rare (145 degrees) or 3 hours for well done (170 degrees).

Yield: 10 to 12 servings

Lemon Butter Steak and Brandy Sauce

1 ½ pounds sirloin steak
1 teaspoon oregano
½ teaspoon seasoned salt
¼ teaspoon pepper
¼ cup butter
2 tablespoons lemon juice

½ teaspoon hot pepper sauce
2 tablespoons Worcestershire sauce
½ cup apricot brandy, heated
Garnishes: lemon slices, fresh parsley

Sprinkle both sides of meat with oregano, salt and pepper; set aside. Melt butter in a heavy skillet over high heat. Stir in lemon juice and hot pepper sauce and add steak and cook quickly until browned on both sides. Reduce heat to medium; cook steak 1 to 2 minutes on each side or until desired degree of doneness is almost reached. Pour in Worcestershire sauce and brandy. Ignite sauce carefully with a grill lighter or long fireplace match. When the flames die, transfer the steak to a serving platter. Spoon sauce over steak and garnish with lemon and parsley. Serve immediately.

Yield: 2 servings

A food is not necessarily essential just because your child hates it.

🍃 Slow Oven-Barbecued Brisket

Unlike a tenderloin steak, brisket is best when thoroughly cooked. It is this advantage that makes brisket excellent for reheating. Do not let the brisket dry out when reheating—moisture keeps the meat tender.

1	(7 to 9-pound) first cut beef brisket	4	large bay leaves, crumbled
1	teaspoon minced garlic	1	(12-ounce) can tomato paste
3	tablespoons freshly ground pepper	1	cup firmly packed dark brown sugar
1	teaspoon celery seeds	1	cup soy sauce
1	teaspoon ground ginger (optional)	½	cup Worcestershire sauce
		2	onions, thinly sliced
			Water, beer or wine

Place brisket on one extra-wide piece (or two regular pieces) of foil, large enough to completely cover and seal in the meat. Rub brisket on all sides with garlic. Combine pepper, celery seed, ginger and bay leaf; sprinkle over beef. Combine tomato paste, sugar, soy sauce and Worcestershire sauce and rub over brisket. Make ¼-inch deep cuts in fat side of brisket with a sharp knife and place onions on top. Wrap foil around brisket and carefully seal. Place brisket, fat side up, on a rack in a roasting pan. Bake at 350 degrees for 4 hours. Carefully open foil to avoid steam and expose the onion-covered top. Bake 1 hour. Remove meat and place on a heated serving platter. Degrease the cooking liquid and stir in a small amount of water, beer or wine. Place pan over medium-high heat; bring to a boil and reduce slightly. To serve, thinly slice brisket against the grain and top with a spoonful of sauce; pass remaining sauce.

Yield: 8 servings

Beef Stroganoff

*This is a great party dish. Serve with a super salad
and good bread and you have an elegant meal.*

2	pounds boneless sirloin or top round	1	(10¾-ounce) can condensed beef broth
	Salt	1	teaspoon Dijon mustard
	Pepper	1	(8-ounce) package mushrooms, sliced
½	cup butter		
4	green onions, sliced	⅓	cup sour cream
5	tablespoons all-purpose flour	⅓	cup Sauternes

Trim meat and slice across the grain into strips ½-inch thick and 2-inches long. Sprinkle strips with salt and pepper. Melt butter in a large skillet over medium-high heat. Add meat strips; sauté, stirring constantly, until browned. Push meat to outer rim of skillet. Add onions to skillet; sauté 5 minutes until tender and light brown. Push onions aside. Stir flour into pan drippings. Cook 1 minute, stirring constantly. Gradually add broth; cook over medium-high heat, stirring constantly, until mixture is thick and bubbly. Reduce heat and stir in mustard and mushrooms. Cover and simmer 1 hour. Recipe can be made ahead and allowed to stand at this point. Stir in sour cream and Sauternes. Cook over medium heat until thoroughly heated (do not boil). Season to taste with salt. Serve with hot cooked rice or noodles.

Yield: 4 to 6 servings

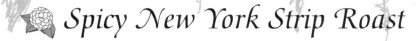 Spicy New York Strip Roast

1	(1 to 1 ¾-pound) New York strip steak (about 3 inches thick)	¼	teaspoon salt
		¼	teaspoon freshly ground pepper
1	teaspoon dried thyme	¼	teaspoon ground red pepper
1	teaspoon dried oregano	1	tablespoon olive oil
1	teaspoon dried rosemary		

Trim excess fat from steak. Combine thyme, oregano, rosemary, salt, pepper and red pepper in a small bowl; crush with the back of a spoon. Press mixture evenly on both sides of steak. Heat oil in a cast-iron skillet over medium-high heat; add steak, and brown 3 minutes on each side. Bake (in skillet) at 450 degrees for 20 to 25 minutes or until desired degree of doneness. Remove from oven; cover with foil, and let stand 10 minutes. Cut into thin slices, to serve.

Yield: 4 to 6 servings

Basting syringes can be used to suck up and remove excess grease from the bottom of a meat loaf pan or when browning chopped meat.

ENTICING ENTRÉES

Rueben Casserole

1 (27-ounce) can sauerkraut, drained
2 tomatoes, thinly sliced
2 tablespoons Thousand Island salad dressing
2 tablespoons butter, cut into small pieces
3 (3-ounce) packages corned beef, shredded
2 cups (8 ounces) shredded Swiss cheese
1 (10-ounce) can refrigerated buttermilk biscuits
2 rye crackers, crumbled
¼ teaspoon caraway seeds

Spread sauerkraut in a lightly greased 13 x 9 x 2-inch baking dish. Arrange tomato slices over sauerkraut. Spread salad dressing over tomato and dot with butter. Top mixture with corned beef and cheese. Bake at 425 degrees for 15 minutes. Separate each biscuit into 3 thin layers; arrange over the top of casserole. Sprinkle with cracker crumbs and caraway. Bake 15 to 20 minutes or until biscuits are golden brown.

Yield: 6 to 8 servings

Note: fresh corned beef may be substituted for packaged corned beef and one slice of dry rye bread, crumbled, may be substituted for rye crackers.

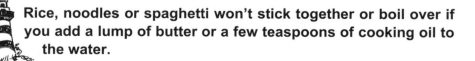

Rice, noodles or spaghetti won't stick together or boil over if you add a lump of butter or a few teaspoons of cooking oil to the water.

Salisbury Burgundy Steaks

1 (10¾-ounce) can beefy mushroom soup, divided	⅓ cup water
1½-2 pounds lean ground beef	¼ cup Burgundy or other dry red wine
¼ cup fine, dry bread crumbs	1 small clove garlic, minced (optional)
1 large egg, lightly beaten	¼ teaspoon dried marjoram
¼ teaspoon salt	Hot cooked noodles
4 slices bacon	

Combine ⅓ cup soup, beef, bread crumbs, egg and salt; stirring until well blended. Shape into 6 oval patties. Cook bacon in a large skillet over medium-high heat until crisp. Remove bacon, crumbled and set aside. Pour off all but 2 tablespoons drippings. Heat drippings over medium-high heat; add patties and brown on both sides. Stir in remaining soup, water, wine, garlic and marjoram. Cover; simmer for 20 minutes or until done, stirring occasionally. Serve over hot cooked noodles and sprinkle with bacon.

Yield: 6 servings

Beef Sherry

2 tablespoons vegetable oil	2 (10¾-ounce) cans golden mushroom soup
2 (8-ounce) packages mushrooms, sliced	1 (10¾-ounce) envelope onion soup mix
3 pounds beef stew meat	¾ cup sherry

Heat oil in a large Dutch oven over medium-high heat; add mushrooms and sauté until tender. Stir in beef, soup, soup mix and sherry. Cover tightly. Bake at 300 degrees for 3 hours. Serve over rice or noodles. Recipe is best if made ahead. Recipe may be frozen and reheated.

Yield: 8 to 10 servings

ENTICING ENTRÉES

Children's Favorite Burger Noodle Bake

Children give this dish a "thumbs-up."

1 (8-ounce) package wide noodles	2 tablespoons sugar
1 ½ pounds lean ground beef	2 tablespoons Worcestershire sauce
⅔ cup finely chopped onions	1 teaspoon salt
2 (10 ¾-ounce) cans tomato soup	½ cup corn flake crumbs
1 (3-ounce) package cream cheese, cut into pieces	1 tablespoon butter or margarine, melted

Cook noodles according to package directions; drain and place in a large bowl. Brown ground beef in a large skillet, stirring until it crumbles; drain. Add onions and cook, stirring often, until tender, but not brown. Stir in soup, cheese, sugar, Worcestershire and salt. Bring to a boil, reduce heat, and simmer 15 minutes, stirring occasionally. Combine noodles and sauce, stirring well. Spoon into a lightly greased 11 x 7 x1 ½-inch baking dish. Combine corn flakes and butter; sprinkle over top. Bake at 350 degrees for 20 minutes.

Yield: 8 servings

ENTICING ENTRÉES

Company's Coming Casserole

1	cup fine noodles	2	(10 ¾-ounce) cans tomato soup
4	slices bacon	1	tablespoon Worcestershire sauce
1	large onion, chopped		
1	green bell pepper, chopped	1	teaspoon salt
1	(8-ounce) package mushrooms	¼	teaspoon dried oregano
2	pounds lean ground beef		

Cook noodles according to package directions; drain and set aside. Cook bacon in a large skillet over medium-high heat until crisp. Remove bacon, crumble and set aside. Pour off all but 2 tablespoons drippings. Add onion, bell pepper and mushrooms to skillet; sauté 5 minutes. Remove from skillet and set aside. Brown ground beef in the skillet, stirring until it crumbles; drain. Combine beef, vegetables, soup and noodles in a large bowl. Spoon mixture into a lightly greased baking dish; sprinkle with bacon. Bake at 325 degrees for 45 minutes or until thoroughly heated.

Yield: 6 to 8 servings

Don't freeze spaghetti, macaroni or noodle mixtures. They tend to lose texture and become too soft when reheated.

 # Southwest Meat Loaf

1 large egg, lightly beaten	½ teaspoons sugar
1 cup salsa, divided	½ teaspoon salt
¾ cup soft bread crumbs	¼ teaspoon ground cinnamon
(about 1 slice)	⅛ teaspoon ground cloves
⅓ cup raisins	1 ½ pounds lean ground beef
¼ cup finely chopped onions	

Combine egg, ¾ cup salsa, bread crumbs, raisins, onion, sugar, salt, cinnamon and cloves in a large bowl. Add beef, mixing well. Spoon mixture into a 9 x 5 x 3-inch loaf pan. Bake at 350 degrees for 1 hour. Spoon remaining ¼ cup salsa on top. Insert meat thermometer and bake until center reaches 160 degrees. Recipe may be made ahead; slice, wrap in foil, and freeze. Thaw and serve warm or cool; great for sandwiches.

Yield: 6 servings

 # Ground Veal "Cutlets"

1 pound lean ground veal	Pepper
½ cup small curd cottage	⅓ cup seasoned dry bread
cheese	crumbs
2 tablespoons fresh minced	2 tablespoons grated Parmesan
parsley	cheese
Salt	Vegetable oil

Combine veal, cottage cheese, parsley, salt and pepper in a bowl, blending well. Shape into 4 or 5 cutlets or burgers. Combine bread crumbs and cheese in a shallow dish. Roll cutlet in crumb mixture, coating each side. Heat oil in a skillet over medium-high heat; sauté cutlets for 5 minutes on each side until browned. Ground turkey may be substituted for veal.

Yield: 4 to 5 servings

Family Casserole

This recipe is the very favorite with the grandchildren. They call ahead of their visit to make sure it is on the dinner table when they arrive.

¼ pound elbow macaroni	1 tablespoon Worcestershire sauce
2 tablespoons vegetable oil	
1 ½ pounds lean ground beef	1 teaspoon salt
1 cup chopped onions	¾ teaspoon chili powder
1 (10-ounce) package frozen mixed vegetables, thawed	Dash pepper
	1 ½ cups (6 ounces) shredded cheddar cheese
2 cups canned tomatoes	
1 cup tomato sauce	

Cook macaroni in boiling, salted water for 6 minutes; drain and set aside. Heat oil in a large skillet over medium-high heat. Add beef and onion; sauté until beef crumbles; drain if desired. Stir in vegetables, tomatoes, tomato sauce, Worcestershire, salt, chili powder and pepper. Stir in macaroni, blending well. Spoon into a lightly greased 2 to 3-quart baking dish. Let stand 1 hour. Bake at 350 degrees, covered for 30 minutes. Uncover, sprinkle with cheese, and bake 30 minutes. Fresh vegetables of your choice may be substituted for frozen. Recipe may be frozen.

Yield: 6 servings

After purchasing, store dried pasta, rice (except brown rice), and whole grains in tightly covered containers in a cool, dry place. Refrigerate brown rice. Refrigerate or freeze grains if they will not be used within five months.

Pastitsio

Fine, dry bread crumbs	½ teaspoon ground cinnamon
12 ounces macaroni	Béchamel Sauce
1 cup chopped onion	1 ½ cups grated Parmesan
1 pound lean ground beef	cheese, divided
1 (10 ¾-ounce) can tomato puree	3 large eggs
1 teaspoon salt	3 cups milk
1 teaspoon pepper	Paprika

Coat a buttered 13 x 9 x 2-inch baking dish on the bottom and up sides with bread crumbs; set aside. Cook macaroni according to package directions; drain and set aside. Combine onion and beef in a large skillet over medium-high heat; cook, stirring constantly, until beef crumbles and onion is tender; drain. Stir in tomato puree, salt, pepper and cinnamon. Bring mixture to a boil; reduce heat, and simmer 20 minutes. Layer half of macaroni, half of Béchamel and ½ cup of cheese in prepared pan. Spoon all of the meat mixture on cheese. Repeat layers of remaining macaroni, Béchamel and ½ cup cheese. Beat together eggs and milk; pour over layered mixture. Insert knife at several places to allow liquid to disperse. Sprinkle with remaining ½ cup cheese and paprika. Bake at 350 degrees for 1 hour or until golden brown and set. Serve warm, not hot. Recipe reheats well.

Yield: 6 to 8 servings

Béchamel Sauce:

¼ cup butter	Salt
¼ cup all-purpose flour	Nutmeg
3 cups milk	

Melt butter in a heavy saucepan over medium heat; add flour, whisking until smooth. Cook 1 minute, whisking constantly. Gradually add milk; cook, whisking constantly, until mixture is thickened and bubbly. Stir in salt and nutmeg.

Yield: 3 ½ cups

Veal Stew

*"It is such a hearty, satisfying dish to
eat when coming inside on a cold, windy day."*

2	tablespoons all-purpose flour	½	cup dry white wine
½	teaspoon salt	1	teaspoon paprika
½	teaspoon freshly ground pepper	1	teaspoon nutmeg
		4	onions, sliced
2	pounds boneless veal shoulder, cut into small cubes	1	clove garlic, finely chopped
		1	tablespoon finely chopped parsley
2	tablespoons butter	1	tablespoon sugar
1	cup chicken stock	1	cup sour cream

Place flour, salt and pepper in a large plastic bag; add veal cubes, shaking to coat each piece completely. Melt butter in a large pot over high heat; add veal and brown on all sides. Reduce heat to low and stir in broth, wine, paprika and nutmeg. Add onions, garlic, parsley and sugar, stirring well. Bake at 300 degrees, covered, for 1 ½ to 2 hours until meat is tender. Stir in sour cream 10 minutes before serving.

Yield: 4 to 6 servings

174

Roast Lamb

1	(5 to 7-pound) leg of lamb		Olive oil
5	cloves garlic, sliced		Salt
	lengthwise		Pepper
	Fresh or dried mint	1	cup water

Cut slits in meat and insert garlic slices and mint. Rub lamb with olive oil and sprinkle with salt and pepper. Place in a roasting pan with 1 cup water. Cover with foil. Bake at 350 degrees for 35 minutes per pound. Remove foil; increase heat to 425 degrees and bake until a meat thermometer registers 140 degrees for rare or to desired degree of doneness.

Yield: 8 to 10 servings

For a delicious addition, add to pan when roast is halfway done: peeled and quartered potatoes that are sprinkled with salt, pepper, oregano, garlic, olive oil, and lemon juice. Roast the same as the lamb for the rest of the time.

Wine Braised Lamb Shanks ✓

3	tablespoons all-purpose flour	2	tablespoons chopped onion
1	teaspoon salt	2	tablespoons chopped garlic
½	teaspoon freshly ground pepper	2	tablespoons grated lemon peel
4	(1-pound) lamb shanks	1	tablespoon lemon juice
2	tablespoons olive oil	½	teaspoon dried thyme
1 ½	cups dry red wine	½	teaspoon rosemary
2	tablespoons chopped fresh parsley		Garnish: chopped fresh parsley

Combine flour, salt and pepper in a shallow dish. Dredge lamb in flour mixture; shaking off excess. Heat oil in a large Dutch oven or soup pot. Add lamb and brown on all sides. Arrange lamb in pot in a single layer; cover. Bake at 350 degrees for 2 hours; drain grease. Combine wine, parsley, onion, garlic, lemon peel, juice, thyme and rosemary in a small bowl; pour over lamb. Bake, covered, for 35 minutes. Garnish with parsley.

Yield: 4 servings

ENTICING ENTRÉES

Moussaka

1	cup fine, dry bread crumbs, divided	1	clove garlic, chopped
2	tablespoons margarine	½	teaspoon dried oregano
2	eggplants, peeled and sliced ½-inch thick	1	teaspoon dried basil
¼	cup butter	1	teaspoon ground cinnamon
2	large onions, chopped		Salt
1 ½	pounds ground lamb		Pepper
2	(8-ounce) cans tomato sauce		Grated Parmesan cheese
			Cream Sauce

Coat a buttered 13 x 9 x 2-inch baking dish on the bottom and up sides with ¼ cup bread crumbs; set aside. Melt margarine in a large skillet over medium-high heat. Add eggplant and sauté until brown on both sides. (You may also brush eggplant slices with melted margarine and broil 5 minutes on each side until brown.) Set aside. Melt butter in a large Dutch oven or soup pot over medium-high heat. Add onions and sauté until tender. Add lamb; cook 10 minutes, stirring frequently, until brown and crumbly; drain. Combine tomato sauce, garlic, oregano, basil, cinnamon, salt and pepper in a bowl; stir into meat mixture. Bring mixture to a boil; reduce heat, and simmer 30 minutes. Stir in ¼ cup bread crumbs. Layer half of eggplant and half of meat sauce in prepared pan; sprinkle layer with cheese and ¼ cup bread crumbs. Repeat layers of eggplant and meat sauce; sprinkle with cheese and remaining crumbs. Pour Cream Sauce on top. Bake at 350 degrees for 1 hour until golden brown. Cool 30 minutes before serving.

Yield: 6 to 8 servings

Cream Sauce:

½	cup butter or margarine	1	(15-ounce) container ricotta or cottage cheese
6	tablespoons all-purpose flour		
4	cups milk	3	large eggs, lightly beaten
		½	teaspoon nutmeg

Melt butter in a saucepan over medium heat; add flour, whisking until smooth. Cook 1 minute, whisking constantly. Gradually add milk; cook, whisking constantly, until mixture is thickened and bubbly. Remove from heat and cool slightly. Stir in ricotta, eggs and nutmeg.

Yield: about 6 cups

Pork Tenderloin Diane

1 (1-pound) pork tenderloin, cut into 10 pieces
2 teaspoon lemon-pepper seasoning
2 tablespoons butter
2 tablespoons lemon juice

1 tablespoon Worcestershire sauce
1 teaspoon Dijon mustard
1 tablespoon finely chopped fresh chives or parsley

Place pork pieces between two sheets of plastic wrap; flatten to 1-inch thick, using a meat mallet. Sprinkle pork on both sides with seasoning. Melt butter in a large skillet over medium-high heat. Add pork and brown 3 to 4 minutes on each side. Transfer pork to a serving platter; cover and keep warm. Stir juice, Worcestershire and mustard into pan juices. Cook, stirring constantly, until thoroughly heated. Pour over pork medallions and sprinkle with chives or parsley.

Yield: 5 small servings

Hawaiian Pork Chops

1 tablespoon canola oil
4 (1 to 1 ½-inch thick) pork chops, trimmed
1 (16-ounce) can beef broth
½ cup pineapple tidbits, undrained

¼ cup chopped green bell pepper
¼ cup ketchup
1 tablespoon vinegar
1 tablespoon light brown sugar
1 tablespoon cornstarch
2 tablespoons water

Heat oil in a large skillet over medium-high heat. Add chops and sauté until browned on both sides; transfer chops to a baking dish. Stir broth, pineapple, bell pepper, ketchup, vinegar and brown sugar into skillet, mixing well. Stir cornstarch into water; stir into broth mixture. Bring to a boil; boil 1 minute until thickened. Pour sauce over chops. Bake at 300 degrees for 2 hours. Serve chops with rice, pouring extra sauce over rice.

Yield: 4 servings

Cranberry-Glazed Pork Chops

*Before sautéing, slightly flour all white meats such as pork,
chicken breasts and veal. This keeps the meat from drying out.*

4	(4-ounce) boneless pork chops	½	cup jellied cranberry sauce
¼	teaspoon pepper	1	tablespoon honey
	Vegetable cooking spray	⅛	teaspoon ground ginger
½	cup chicken broth	⅛	ground cinnamon

Sprinkle both sides of pork chops with pepper. Spray a heavy skillet with cooking spray; place over medium-high heat until hot. Add pork chops; sauté 3 minutes on each side until golden brown.

Add chicken broth; cover. Cook over medium heat for 12 to 15 minutes or until chops are tender, turning once. Combine cranberry sauce, honey, ginger and cinnamon in a small bowl, stirring to blend. Pour mixture over chops. Cook 1 minute, turning to glaze both sides. Place chops on a serving platter; top with cranberry mixture. Glaze is also good on ham, chicken or roast pork.

Yield: 4 servings

Ham-Stuffed Green Peppers

6	medium green bell peppers	½	cup soft bread crumbs
2	eggs, lightly beaten	¼	cup finely chopped celery
1 ½	cups whole kernel corn, fresh or canned	2	tablespoons melted butter
1 ½	cups diced cooked ham	1	tablespoon finely chopped onion
1	cup chopped tomatoes	1	teaspoon salt

Slice tops from peppers; core and remove seeds. Cook peppers in boiling, salted water to cover for 3 to 5 minutes; drain well. Combine eggs, corn, ham, tomatoes, bread crumbs, celery, butter, onion and salt in a large bowl. Spoon mixture evenly into pepper shells. Place peppers upright in a greased baking dish. Pour in a small amount of water; cover with foil. Bake at 350 degrees for 50 to 60 minutes. Recipe may be frozen and reheated.

Yield: 6 servings

ENTICING ENTRÉES

Pork Au Vin

1	tablespoon vegetable oil	1	cup dry red wine
1	pound boneless loin or chops, cut into ¾-inch slices	1	tablespoon Dijon mustard
8	small onions, peeled	2	tablespoons chopped fresh parsley
1	(8-ounce) package mushrooms, halved	1	tablespoon water
1	cup chicken broth or bouillon	1	teaspoon cornstarch

Heat oil in a large skillet over medium-high heat. Add pork; sauté until golden brown on both sides. Remove pork from skillet. Add onions to skillet; sauté, stirring constantly, until golden brown. Remove onions from skillet. Add mushrooms to skillet; cook, stirring constantly, until golden brown. Return pork and onions to pan. Stir in broth, wine and mustard. Bring mixture to a boil; reduce heat, and simmer, covered, for 12 to 15 minutes. Stir in parsley. Remove pork and vegetables and place on a serving platter. Combine water and cornstarch in a small cup; stir into pan juices. Bring to a boil; boil 1 minute until thickened. Pour sauce over pork and vegetables.

Yield: 4 servings

Sweet-Sour Pork Chops Oriental

2	tablespoons vegetable oil	1	tablespoon soy sauce
4-6	loin or rib pork chops	1	teaspoon brown sugar
¾	cup minced onion	¼	teaspoon curry powder
1	clove garlic, minced	¼	teaspoon pepper
1	tablespoon cornstarch	3	small strips lemon peel
1	cup pineapple juice	⅓	cup chopped walnuts
3	tablespoons tomato sauce		Pineapple Rice
2	tablespoons vinegar		

Heat oil in a large skillet over medium-high heat. Add chops and sauté until golden brown on both sides. Transfer chops to a large baking dish. Drain skillet, reserving 1 tablespoon oil in skillet. Heat oil in skillet. Add onions and garlic; sauté until golden brown. Combine cornstarch and pineapple juice; pour into skillet. Stir in tomato sauce, vinegar, soy sauce, brown sugar, curry powder, pepper and lemon peel. Cook over low heat 5 minutes, stirring constantly. Pour mixture over chops and cover. Bake at 350 degrees for 30 minutes. Sprinkle walnuts over chops, cover, and bake 30 minutes. Serve with Pineapple Rice.

Yield: 4 servings

Pineapple Rice:

1 ⅓	cups rice	¼	cup firmly packed light brown sugar
1 ¼	cups water		
1	(8-ounce) can pineapple chunks, undrained	2	tablespoons butter
		½	teaspoon salt
		6	whole cloves

Combine rice, water, pineapple, brown sugar, butter, salt and cloves in a medium bowl. Spoon into a 1-quart baking dish; cover with foil. Bake at 450 degrees for 20 minutes.

Yield: 4 servings

Pork Tenderloin with Red Onion Confit

1 ½-2	pounds pork tenderloin	2	tablespoons olive oil
2	teaspoons salt		Red Onion Confit
1	tablespoon fresh thyme or		
	1 teaspoon dried		

Place pork in a baking dish; rub with salt, thyme and olive oil. Cover and marinate at room temperature for 30 minutes. Grill pork over medium-hot coals for 15 to 20 minutes or until a meat thermometer registers 155 degrees. Let stand 5 to 10 minutes before thinly slicing. Serve slices on a bed of Red Onion Confit.

Yield: 4 to 6 servings

Red Onion Confit:

2	tablespoons olive oil	¼	teaspoon salt
4	large red onions, thinly sliced	¼	cup balsamic vinegar
2	tablespoons sugar	2	tablespoons crème de cassis
¾	cup dry red wine	1 ½	teaspoons fresh thyme or
¼	cup currants		½ teaspoon dried

Heat olive oil in an enamel or other non-reactive saucepan over medium-low heat. Add onions and sauté 5 to 7 minutes or until softened, but not brown. Stir in sugar, wine and currants. Bring mixture to a boil; reduce heat, and simmer 20 minutes or until nearly all liquid is gone. Stir in vinegar, crème de cassis and thyme. Cook, stirring often for 10 minutes or until onions turn deep golden brown. Serve warm or at room temperature.

Yield: 4 to 6 servings

Pungent Pork Loin Roast

2	tablespoons chopped fresh sage	1	tablespoon fennel seed
2	tablespoons chopped fresh rosemary	1	tablespoon olive oil
1 ½	tablespoons kosher salt	10	cloves garlic
1	tablespoon black peppercorns	1	(5-pound) center loin pork roast
			Apple Bread Dressing

Combine sage, rosemary, salt, peppercorns, fennel, oil and garlic in a food processor; process until mixture forms a paste. Trim excess fat from pork. Make 4 or 5 slits in top of roast and fill each with 1 teaspoon paste mixture. Spread remaining paste over top of roast. Place roast on a rack in a shallow roasting pan. Bake at 325 degrees for 30 to 35 minutes per pound (2 ½ hours) until meat thermometer registers 170 degrees (well done). Serve with Apple Bread Dressing.

Yield: 10 servings

Apple Bread Dressing:

¼	cup butter	¼	teaspoon dried thyme
½	cup chopped onions	¼	teaspoon dried sage
3	cups Granny Smith apples, cored and chopped	⅛	teaspoon pepper
		4	cups bread cubes
2	tablespoon sugar	¼	cup chopped fresh parsley
1	teaspoon salt	2	tablespoon apple cider

Melt butter in a large skillet over medium-high heat. Add onions and sauté until tender. Stir in apples, sugar, salt, thyme, sage and pepper. Cover and cook over low heat until apples are soft. Combine apple mixture, bread cubes, parsley and cider in a large bowl, tossing to blend. Spoon into a lightly greased baking dish; cover with foil. Bake at 325 degrees for 1 hour.

ENTICING ENTRÉES

New York Spaghetti Pie

8	ounces thin spaghetti	1	(8-ounce) container sour cream
2	large eggs	1	pound bulk Italian sausage or
¼- ½	cup grated Parmesan cheese		link sausage, skin removed
	Vegetable cooking spray	1	(6-ounce) can tomato paste
¼- ½	cup butter or margarine	⅓	cup water
1	large onion, chopped		Oregano
1	large green bell pepper, chopped		Garlic powder
			Pepper
1	(8-ounce) package mushrooms, sliced	4	cups (16 ounces) shredded mozzarella cheese

Cook spaghetti according to package directions; drain and place in a large mixing bowl. Beat eggs and Parmesan together; stir into pasta, tossing to coat. Press mixture into the bottom and up sides of a 13 x 9 x 2-inch baking pan coated with cooking spray; set aside. Melt butter in a large skillet over medium-high heat. Add onion, bell pepper and mushrooms and sauté 3 to 5 minutes. Add sour cream, stirring until blended. Pour over spaghetti, spreading up sides. Brown sausage in a skillet over medium-high heat until crumbly; drain well. Stir in tomato paste, water, oregano, garlic powder and pepper. Spread over sour cream mixture; cover with foil. Bake at 350 degrees for 40 minutes; remove foil. Sprinkle with cheese and bake, uncovered, until cheese melts.

Yield: 8 to 10 servings

Pork Chops Creole

4	medium-thick pork chops	2	teaspoons salt
3	cups boiling water	¼	teaspoon dried marjoram
6	bouillon cubes	¼	teaspoon pepper
1	large onion	1	tomato, cut into 4 slices
1	cup rice	4	green bell pepper slices

Heat electric skillet to 220 degrees. Add pork chops and brown on both sides. Remove from pan; set aside. Add water and bouillon cubes to pan, stirring until cubes are dissolved. Slice onion, reserving 4 slices from the center. Chop remaining part of onion. Add rice, chopped onion, salt, marjoram and pepper to pan; stir well to blend. Place chops on rice and top each with a slice of onion, tomato and green pepper ring. Cover and cook 45 minutes, adding more boiling water, if necessary.

Yield: 4 servings

German Feast

1	pound ground pork	1	(16-ounce) can sauerkraut, rinsed and drained
½	teaspoon dried sage		
	Salt	3	cooking apples, peeled, cored and thinly sliced
	Pepper		
4	potatoes, sliced	1	teaspoon fennel seed
1	large onion, thinly sliced	1	cup chicken broth
		2	cloves garlic, minced

Brown pork in a large, deep pan over medium-high heat, stirring until mixture crumbles; drain. Stir in sage, salt and pepper; remove from heat. Layer pork with half of potatoes, half of onion, half of sauerkraut and half of apple slices. Repeat layers and sprinkle with fennel. Combine chicken broth and garlic; pour into pan. Cover and cook over medium heat for 40 minutes.

Yield: 8 servings

Sweet and Sour Pork

2 large eggs, lightly beaten	1 green bell pepper, cut into large pieces
½ cup plus 1 teaspoon all-purpose flour, divided	1 clove garlic, chopped
¼ cup soy sauce, divided	¾ cup sugar
Vegetable oil	⅓ cup vinegar
1 ½ pounds boneless pork loin, cut into cubes	1 (8-ounce) can crushed pineapple, undrained
1 onion, cut into large pieces	1 (8-ounce) can pineapple chunks, drained

Combine eggs, ½ cup flour and 2 tablespoons soy sauce in a shallow bowl. Heat oil in a large skillet over medium-high heat. Dip pork in flour mixture and fry until crisp. Remove from pan and set aside. Add onion, bell pepper and garlic to skillet; cook until tender. Transfer vegetables and pork to a large Dutch oven or soup pot. Combine sugar, vinegar, 2 tablespoons soy sauce, 1 teaspoon flour and crushed pineapple with juice in a blender. Process until well blended. Stir into pork mixture. Stir pineapple chunks into pork mixture. Bring mixture to a boil; reduce heat, and simmer 30 minutes. Serve over hot, cooked rice.

Yield: 6 servings

Vegetables & Side Dishes

Verily, a host of yummy veggies and side dishes to tempt discerning taste buds.

A silhouetted Palmetto, South Carolina's official state tree, was captured from the edge of Mariner's Cove looking towards the mainland. Long a natural part of South Carolina history, it symbolizes a defeat of the British fleet during the American Revolution by a sea island fort built of spongy Palmetto logs. Also known as the Sabal Palmetto, or more commonly the Cabbage Palmetto, it's found on both our State Flag and State Seal.

The following recipe for Cabbage Palmetto was old when printed in a small private 1928 collection of Low Country receipts.

"The Carolina Housewife, long out of print, gives this receipt for a great delicacy. The "cabbage" or heart of the palmetto tree is an ivory-like substance, which is occasionally offered for sale when palmetto groves have been cleared away. It's a rare delicacy, and eating fresh hearts of palmettos is in the class with dining on pheasants' tongues.

The cabbage or heart must be trimmed and only the very tender part used. It is then boiled for two hours, during which time the water must be changed three times, so that the bitter quality will be extracted. When quite soft, pour off the water, and mash the "cabbage" with a wooden or silver spoon. Add one large tablespoon of fresh butter, a little salt and pepper, and reheat with a gill* of cream. Or it may be served cold as a salad with French dressing."

A gill is equal to four fluid ounces.

The recipes in *Vegetables & Side Dishes* don't require a tree to make a dish, and your family will relish every morsel.

Vegetables & Side Dishes

Vegetables & Side Dishes

🌸 **Quick and Easy Recipes are designated with a camellia flower.**
🍃 **Memorable Menu Recipes are designated with a leaf.**

Broccoli à l'Orange

2 (10-ounce) packages frozen broccoli spears, thawed	2 teaspoons cornstarch
¼ cup butter or margarine	1 tablespoon cold water
2 teaspoons grated orange peel	½ teaspoon salt
½ cup fresh orange juice	1 tablespoon chopped pecans

Cook broccoli according to package directions; drain. Arrange broccoli on a serving platter; cover and keep warm. Melt butter in a saucepan over medium-high heat. Add orange peel and juice. Bring mixture to a boil; reduce heat to medium, and simmer 2 minutes. Combine cornstarch and water; stir into orange mixture. Bring to a boil; boil 1 minute, stirring constantly until thick and translucent. Stir in salt. Drizzle sauce over broccoli and sprinkle with pecans. Serve immediately.

Yield: 6 servings

Asparagus Meringue

2 pounds fresh asparagus, trimmed	1 teaspoon lemon juice
¾ cup mayonnaise	4 egg whites (room temperature)
¼ cup sour cream	½ teaspoon salt
1 ½ teaspoons Dijon mustard	½ teaspoon pepper

Cook asparagus in boiling water to cover 6 to 8 minutes or until crisp-tender; drain. Arrange asparagus on an ovenproof platter, alternating tips. Combine mayonnaise, sour cream, mustard and lemon juice in a large bowl; set aside. Beat egg whites until foamy; add salt and pepper. Beat until soft peaks form. Fold egg whites into mayonnaise mixture. Spoon over asparagus, leaving tips exposed. Bake at 375 degrees for 10 minutes.

Yield: 6 servings

Hilton Head Island Deep Well Project Vegetable Lasagna for a Crowd

1	pound lasagna noodles	2	cups broccoli florets
	Olive or vegetable oil (for noodles)	1	teaspoon dried oregano
		1	teaspoon dried basil
¼	cup olive or vegetable oil, divided		Salt
			Pepper
1	cup chopped onion	2	pounds ricotta cheese
1	clove garlic, chopped	3	large eggs
2	(10-ounce) packages frozen chopped spinach, thawed and squeezed dry	3	cups shredded mozzarella cheese
1	pound yellow squash, sliced	1	cup grated Parmesan cheese
8	ounces mushrooms, sliced		Tomato Sauce

Cook noodles in salted and oiled boiling water according to package directions. Drain and coat with oil to prevent sticking; set aside. Heat 2 tablespoons oil in a large skillet over medium-high heat. Add onion and garlic; sauté until tender. Stir in spinach and sauté for 3 minutes. Transfer to a mixing bowl; let cool. Heat remaining 2 tablespoons oil in skillet over medium-high heat. Add squash, mushrooms and broccoli. Sauté until just tender; drain excess liquid. Stir in oregano, basil, salt and pepper; set aside. Stir ricotta cheese and eggs into cooled spinach mixture; set aside. Combine mozzarella and Parmesan; set aside. Layer ingredients evenly in two, 13 x 9 x 2-inch baking dishes in the following order: sauce, noodles, ricotta mixture, vegetables, sauce, noodles, ricotta mixture, cheese mixture, sauce, noodles, sauce and cheese. In each pan there will be 4 layers of sauce, 3 layers of noodles, 2 layers of ricotta-spinach mixture, 1 layer of vegetables and 2 layers of cheese. Bake at 350 degrees for 40 minutes or until hot and bubbly.

Yield: 16 servings (8 large pieces per pan)

VEGETABLES & SIDE DISHES

Tomato Sauce:

¼ cup vegetable oil
1 ¼ cups chopped onion
4 cloves garlic, chopped
42 ounces canned tomatoes, undrained
18 ounces tomato paste

3 cups water
1 ½ teaspoons dried basil
1 ½ teaspoons dried oregano
¾ teaspoon salt
2 bay leaves

Heat oil in a large soup pot over medium heat. Add onion and garlic; sauté until tender. Stir in tomatoes with liquid, tomato paste, water, basil, oregano, salt and bay leaves. Bring to a boil; reduce heat and simmer, covered, for 1 ½ hours.

The Bargain Box is so representative of the total community spirit that has existed on Hilton Head in its recent history. What wonderful services are offered in so many different ways to help so many on our Island!

All of us have seen the long lines of people waiting to get the best bargains on the Island. Many of your customers are our clients, and they struggle every day with the basic necessities of living. We at Deep Well are so appreciative for our partnership with The Bargain Box in providing clothing at no charge for our clients who cannot afford even Bargain Box prices. This prevents duplication of services, and allows both of our organizations to work more efficiently. If Deep Well had to store and sort clothing, we would need an additional storage unit and a lot more volunteers to take care of the extra duties.

What so many of your customers and others in our community don't realize is that The Bargain Box turns around and gives its sales earnings back to the community. Deep Well and other grass roots charitable organizations are the recipients of generous grants that allow most of us to stay in the business of helping those in need on our Island. Without The Bargain Box, The Deep Well Project could not meet its yearly budget. We in turn use our Bargain Box grant to ensure that every Islander has the basic necessities of life.

So, Happy Birthday, Bargain Box! Our Island and its people are much better because of your existence.

Betsy Doughtie
Director, The Deep Well Project

Broccoli and Cauliflower with Shrimp Sauce

1 bunch broccoli, cut into florets	1 small to medium head cauliflower, cut into florets Shrimp Sauce

Cook broccoli and cauliflower in boiling water to cover until crisp-tender; drain. Place cauliflower in a slightly deep vegetable dish, surrounded by broccoli. Pour Shrimp Sauce in the center.

Yield: 8 servings

Shrimp Sauce:

1 (10¾-ounce) can cream of shrimp soup	1 tablespoon lemon juice
1 (3-ounce) package cream cheese with chives	1 (4½-ounce) can small shrimp, rinsed and drained
	½ cup slivered almonds, toasted

Combine soup, cream cheese and juice in a saucepan over medium heat. Cook, stirring constantly, until cheese melts. Stir in shrimp and almonds.

Yield: about 2 cups

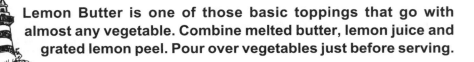 **Lemon Butter is one of those basic toppings that go with almost any vegetable. Combine melted butter, lemon juice and grated lemon peel. Pour over vegetables just before serving.**

Celery and Water Chestnut Casserole

4	cups celery, cut into 1-inch slices		Salt
1	(10¾-ounce) can cream of chicken soup		Pepper
1	(5-ounce) can sliced water chestnuts	¼	cup soft bread crumbs or crushed buttery crackers
1	(2-ounce) jar diced pimientos	¼	cup slivered almonds
		2	tablespoons butter, melted

Cook celery in boiling, salted water to cover for 8 minutes or until crisp-tender; drain. Combine celery, soup, water chestnuts and pimientos. Season to taste with salt and pepper. Spoon mixture into a lightly greased 1½-quart casserole dish. Combine crumbs, almonds and butter; sprinkle over casserole. Bake at 350 degrees for 35 minutes or until golden brown and thoroughly heated.

Yield: 6 servings

# Golden Carrots Supreme

You'll win new friends to carrots if you use this simple French recipe.

¾	cup chicken broth	⅛	teaspoon pepper
¼	cup butter	5	cups diagonally sliced carrots
2	teaspoons sugar	2	teaspoons lemon juice
1	teaspoon salt	¼	cup chopped fresh parsley

Heat chicken broth to boiling in a large saucepan over medium-high heat. Add butter, sugar, salt and pepper, stirring until butter melts. Stir in carrots; cover and simmer for 10 minutes until carrots are crisp-tender. Stir in lemon juice and parsley.

Yield: 7 to 8 servings.

VEGETABLES & SIDE DISHES

Bleu Cheese Pasta

8 ounces penne pasta	1 (15-ounce) can Italian-style
1 tablespoon olive oil	stewed tomatoes
1 large onion, thinly sliced	¼ cup sour cream
½ cup chicken bouillon	¼ cup crumbled blue cheese

Cook pasta according to package directions; drain. Place pasta in serving bowl; cover and keep warm. Heat oil in a large skillet over medium-high heat. Add onion and sauté until tender. Stir in bouillon and tomatoes. Bring mixture to a boil; reduce heat, and simmer 15 minutes. Stir in sour cream and cheese. Stir sauce into pasta, tossing to coat. Shrimp or chicken strips can be added, if desired.

Yield: 4 servings

Barley Casserole

½ cup butter	1 (3-ounce) can sliced
1 cup quick-cooking fine pearl	mushrooms, drained or
barley	1 cup fresh mushrooms,
1 onion, chopped	sautéed
2 cups chicken broth	1 (2-ounce) envelope onion
½ cup slivered almonds	soup mix
1 (5-ounce) can sliced water	
chestnuts, drained	

Heat ½ cup butter in a saucepan over medium-high heat. Stir in barley and onion. Sauté, stirring constantly, until light golden brown. Stir in broth, almonds, water chestnuts, mushrooms and soup mix. Pour mixture into a lightly greased casserole dish. Bake at 350 degrees for 1 hour.

Yield: 6 servings

Barley is one of humanity's oldest grains. It is delicious and accompanies chicken, turkey or pork. Barley can be cooked a day or two ahead and refrigerated before baking in other recipes. Leftovers freeze well.

Danish Red Cabbage

The flavor improves when prepared the day before
being served. Delicious with pork roast or turkey.

¼ cup butter	2 tablespoons currant jelly or
3 pounds red cabbage, coarsely	grape jelly and lemon juice
shredded	1 tablespoon sugar
½ cup water	1 teaspoon salt
¼ cup vinegar	

Melt butter in a large saucepan over medium-high heat. Add cabbage, tossing to coat. Stir in water and vinegar. Cover and cook 10 minutes or until cabbage is barely tender. Combine jelly, sugar and salt in a small bowl; stir into cabbage mixture. Cover and cook 5 minutes.

 A lump of sugar added to the water when cooking vegetable greens helps retain their fresh color.

 # Spinach Casserole

2 (10-ounce) packages frozen	Salt
chopped spinach, thawed	Pepper
6 ounces cream cheese with	1 cup herb-seasoned stuffing
chives and onions, softened	mix
6 tablespoons butter, divided	

Cook spinach according to package directions; drain very well. Combine cream cheese, 4 tablespoons butter, salt and pepper in a large bowl. Stir in spinach. Spoon mixture into lightly greased casserole dish. Melt remaining 2 tablespoons butter and mix with stuffing mix. Sprinkle over spinach mixture. Bake at 350 degrees, uncovered, for 30 minutes.

Yield: 4 to 6 servings

VEGETABLES & SIDE DISHES

Garden Casserole

*This is a nutritious recipe that tastes great and
uses many garden vegetables. The brown rice gives it a
nutlike flavor and the cashews add crunch.*

3	cups chicken broth	2	cloves garlic
1 ½	cups uncooked brown rice	1	bunch broccoli, cut into florets
2	large onions, chopped, divided	1	head cauliflower, cut into florets
3	tablespoons low-sodium soy sauce	2	red bell peppers, cut into strips
2	tablespoons butter, melted	1	cup toasted cashews
½	teaspoon dried thyme	2	cups (8 ounces) shredded cheddar cheese
	Salt		
3	tablespoons vegetable oil		

Combine broth, rice, half of onion, soy sauce and butter in a 3-quart casserole
dish; cover. Bake at 350 degrees for 50 to 60 minutes or until rice is cooked.
Stir in thyme and season to taste with salt. Keep oven heated. Heat oil in a
large skillet over high heat. Add remaining onion, garlic, broccoli, cauliflower
and bell pepper. Sauté for 5 minutes. Pour vegetables over rice mixture; cover.
Bake 10 minutes; remove lid. Sprinkle with cashews. Place cheese in mounds
around edges. Bake 5 minutes or until cheese melts.

Yield: 6 servings

**Never salt vegetables during cooking. The salt draws out the
liquid and the vegetables won't cook evenly.**

Baked Corn Pudding ✓

⅓ cup butter or margarine	1½ teaspoons baking powder
1 tablespoon all-purpose flour	1 (15-ounce) can cream-style corn
½ cup evaporated milk	
2 large eggs, lightly beaten	1 (15-ounce) can whole kernel corn, drained
½ cup sugar	

Melt butter in a large skillet over medium heat; add flour, whisking until smooth. Cook 1 minute, whisking constantly. Gradually add milk, eggs, sugar and baking powder, stirring until well blended. Stir in corn; pour mixture into a lightly greased 1½-quart casserole dish. Bake at 350 degrees for 40 minutes or until knife inserted in the center comes out clean.

 # Green Beans Oriental

2 (10-ounce) packages frozen French-style green beans, thawed	1 onion, grated
	½ cup (2 ounces) shredded cheddar cheese
1 tablespoon vegetable oil	
1 (8-ounce) package mushrooms, sliced	2 teaspoons soy sauce
	1 teaspoon hot pepper sauce
2 (10¾-ounce) cans cream of celery soup	Salt
	1 (3½-ounce) can French-fried onions
1 (15-ounce) can bean sprouts, drained	

Cook beans according to package directions; drain and place in a large bowl. Heat oil in a skillet over medium-high heat. Add mushrooms and sauté until tender; drain, if necessary. Add mushrooms, soups, sprouts, grated onion, cheese, soy sauce and pepper sauce to beans, stirring until well blended. Season to taste with salt. Pour into a lightly greased 2-quart casserole dish; top with French-fried onions. Bake at 350 degrees for 1 hour.

Yield: 8 servings

Vidalia Onions Au Gratin

2	large Vidalia onions, sliced		Salt
¾	cup chicken broth		Pepper
3	tablespoons melted butter, divided	½	cup soft, fresh bread crumbs
¼	teaspoon dried thyme	¼	cup (2 ounces) shredded sharp cheddar cheese

Arrange onion slices overlapping in a lightly greased 8 x 8-inch baking dish. Pour broth and 1½ tablespoons butter over onions; sprinkle with thyme, salt and pepper. Bake at 400 degrees for 25 minutes. Combine bread crumbs and remaining melted butter; stir in cheese. Sprinkle on casserole and bake 10 minutes.

Yield: 6 servings

 A little vinegar or lemon juice added to potatoes before draining will make them extra white when mashed.

 *Roasted Potato Medley*

5	russet potatoes (about 1¼ pounds)	1	tablespoon chopped fresh thyme or 1 teaspoon dried
3	sweet potatoes (about 1½ pounds)	½	teaspoon salt
3	tablespoons olive oil	½	teaspoon cracked black pepper

Peel potatoes and cut into ½-inch slices. Place slices in a single layer on a lightly greased 15 x 10-inch jelly-roll pan. Brush both sides with oil. Bake at 500 degrees on bottom rack of oven for about 8 minutes on each side. (Watch closely and remove if starting to over-brown.) Sprinkle potatoes with thyme, salt and pepper. Serve immediately.

Yield: 6 to 8 servings

VEGETABLES & SIDE DISHES

🍃 *Sweet Potato Casserole* ✓

*"A sweet potato casserole is so sweet,
it's like having dessert with dinner."*

3 cups grated sweet potatoes	¼ cup evaporated milk
2 large eggs, lightly beaten	1 teaspoon vanilla extract
½ cup butter, softened	¼ teaspoon ground cinnamon
½ cup sugar	⅛ teaspoon nutmeg
¼ cup firmly packed light brown sugar	

Topping:

1 cup crushed cornflake cereal	¼ cup pecans, chopped (optional)
2 tablespoons butter, melted	Sherry (optional)
½ cup firmly packed light brown sugar	

Combine potatoes, eggs, butter, sugar, brown sugar, milk, vanilla, cinnamon and nutmeg in a large bowl, stirring until well blended. Spoon into a lightly greased 1 ½ to 2-quart casserole dish. Combine cornflakes, butter, brown sugar and pecans in a small bowl; sprinkle over casserole. Bake at 450 degrees for 15 to 20 minutes. Sprinkle with a splash of sherry, if desired.

Yield: 8 servings

Line the bottom of the vegetable compartments with paper towels. This absorbs the excess moisture and keeps your fruits and vegetables fresh longer.

Roasted Veggies

⅓ cup olive oil	6-8 cups cubed vegetables such
¼ cup balsamic vinegar	as: eggplant, onion,
1 ½ tablespoons soy sauce	zucchini, red or yellow
1 tablespoon chopped fresh	peppers, sweet potatoes or
basil or rosemary	any squash

Combine olive oil, vinegar, soy sauce and basil in a very large bowl. Add vegetables, tossing to coat. Cover and marinate 1 hour. Pour vegetables and marinade in a large, shallow roasting pan. Bake at 400 degrees for 45 to 50 minutes, stirring every 20 minutes. Serve hot, cold or at room temperature.

Yield: 6 to 8 servings

Easy Eggplant Casserole

1 large eggplant, peeled and diced	1 teaspoon salt
	½ teaspoon garlic salt
1 tablespoon vegetable oil	Pepper
1 large onion	2 tablespoons bacon drippings
1 large egg, lightly beaten	or melted butter
1 tablespoon Worcestershire sauce	1 cup fine, dry bread crumbs
	1 cup (4 ounces) shredded cheese, divided

Cook eggplant in boiling, salted water to cover until tender; drain and mash. Heat oil in a skillet over medium-high heat; add onion and sauté until tender. Combine eggplant, onion, egg, Worcestershire, salt, garlic salt and pepper in a large bowl. Melt drippings or butter and pour into the bottom of an 8 x 8-inch casserole dish. Arrange layers of eggplant, crumbs and ¾ cup cheese. Bake at 350 degrees for 20 minutes. Sprinkle top with remaining ¼ cup cheese; bake 10 minutes.

Yield: 6 servings

Peas with Prosciutto

3 tablespoons olive oil	2 tablespoons finely chopped
2 cloves garlic, sliced	parsley
2 tablespoons finely chopped	Salt
prosciutto	Pepper
1 (10-ounce) package frozen	
peas, thawed	

Heat oil in a skillet over low heat; add garlic and sauté until garlic just turns golden brown. Remove garlic from skillet. Add prosciutto and sauté until it begins to crisp. Stir in peas, parsley, salt and pepper. Cover and cook 5 minutes or until peas are tender.

Yield: 4 to 6 servings

Home-Style Squash Casserole ✓

2 pounds yellow squash,	1 teaspoon salt
coarsely chopped (4 cups)	½ teaspoon pepper
¼ cup melted butter, divided	2 large eggs, lightly beaten
½ cup chopped onion	½ cup cracker crumbs
2 teaspoons sugar	

Cook squash in boiling water to cover for 8 minutes or until tender. Drain and mash in a large bowl, discarding any liquid that accumulates. Combine 3 tablespoons melted butter and onion in a skillet over medium-high heat; sauté for 5 minutes or until tender. Stir onion mixture into squash. Add sugar, salt, pepper and eggs, stirring until well blended. Pour mixture into a lightly greased 2-quart casserole dish. Sprinkle crumbs over top and drizzle with remaining 1 tablespoon butter. Bake at 350 degrees for 20 to 30 minutes or until top is golden brown and edges are bubbly.

Yield: 8 servings

VEGETABLES & SIDE DISHES

✓ Tomatoes with Dill Sauce

½	cup sour cream	¼	teaspoon seasoned salt
¼	cup mayonnaise	6	firm, ripe tomatoes
2	tablespoons chopped fresh chives		Salt
			Pepper
4	teaspoons dill pickle juice or fresh dill weed		

Combine sour cream, mayonnaise, chives, juice and salt in a small bowl; set aside. Slice tomatoes in half and sprinkle with salt and pepper. Place tomatoes, cut side up, on a broiler pan. Broil tomatoes for 3 to 5 minutes until thoroughly heated (do not turn over). Spoon sauce over hot tomatoes. Serve immediately.

Yield: 6 to 12 servings

🌼 Wild Rice Casserole

1	cup cubed cheddar cheese	¼	cup olive oil
1	cup cubed processed American cheese loaf	1	(28-ounce) can tomatoes, cut into pieces with liquid
½	cup minced onion		Butter
½	cup minced green bell pepper		Salt
1	cup wild rice		Pepper
1	cup black olives, sliced	1	cup boiling water
1	cup canned mushrooms and liquid		

Layer cheddar cheese, process cheese, onion, bell pepper, wild rice, olives, mushrooms with liquid, olive oil and tomatoes with liquid in the order listed in a 3-quart casserole dish. Do not stir. Dot with butter and sprinkle with salt and pepper. Pour water over casserole and cover with foil. Bake at 350 degrees for 1 ½ hours. Uncover; reduce heat to 325 degrees and bake for 30 minutes. Let stand, covered, for 15 minutes before serving.

Yield: 10 servings

Mozzarella Potato Pie

1 ¾ pounds potatoes, peeled	3 tomatoes, peeled and sliced
½ cup melted butter or margarine, divided	1 teaspoon dried oregano or Italian seasoning
Salt	1 teaspoon dried basil
Pepper	½ cup grated Parmesan cheese
8 ounces sliced mozzarella cheese, divided	

Cook potatoes in boiling, salted water to cover until tender. Drain and mash in a large bowl. Stir in ¼ cup butter and season to taste with salt and pepper. Spread potatoes in a lightly greased 10-inch pie plate. Arrange half of mozzarella slices on top of potatoes. Top with tomato slices and sprinkle with oregano and basil. Layer remaining mozzarella slices with Parmesan cheese over pie. Drizzle with remaining ¼ cup melted butter (you may spray top with butter-flavored cooking spray instead). Bake at 425 degrees for 20 to 25 minutes or until golden brown.

Yield: 6 to 8 servings

Rice and Corn Dressing

¼ cup butter	1 (15-ounce) can whole kernel corn with peppers
1 large onion, chopped	1 cup chopped nuts
½ cup chopped celery	2 (11 ½-ounce) cans chicken broth
½ cup chopped green pepper	Salt
½ cup minced fresh parsley	Pepper
2 cups uncooked rice	

Melt butter in a large Dutch oven or soup pot over medium-high heat. Add onion, celery, bell pepper and parsley; sauté until tender. Stir in rice and cook until grains are slightly brown. Stir in corn and nuts, mixing well. Add broth, cover, and cook over low heat until liquid is absorbed and rice is tender. Season to taste with salt and pepper.

Yield: 8 servings

Fluffy Turnips

*"We think of cooked dishes when we think of turnips,
but they are delicious raw—thinly sliced or grated in salads."*

6-8 turnips, peeled and quartered	**3 tablespoons butter**
Boiling water	**1 teaspoon grated onion**
1 ½ teaspoons salt	**Paprika**
2 teaspoons chicken bouillon granules	**Garnish: chopped fresh parsley**

Place turnips in boiling water to cover with 1 ½ teaspoons salt for each quart of water used. Stir in bouillon granules. Bring mixture to a boil; reduce heat, and simmer, covered, until turnips are tender. Drain and mash in a large mixing bowl. Stir in butter, onion and paprika. Beat turnip mixture at medium-high speed with an electric mixture until fluffy. Spoon into a serving bowl and garnish with parsley.

Yield: 6 to 8 servings

 # Crock Pot Macaroni and Cheese

An old favorite revisited.

8 ounces elbow macaroni	**1 ½ cups milk**
½ cup butter or margarine, melted	**3-4 cups (12 to 16 ounces) shredded sharp cheddar cheese**
2 large eggs, lightly beaten	**Salt**
1 (12-ounce) can evaporated milk	**Pepper**

Cook macaroni according to package directions; drain. Combine macaroni, butter, eggs, evaporated milk, milk, cheese, salt and pepper in a crock pot, stirring to blend. Cook on LOW for 2 hours.

Yield: 6 to 8 servings

Kidney Bean, Artichoke and Mushroom Casserole

"Serve this to your vegetarian friends and they will adore you."

1 cup dried red kidney beans	1 ¾ cups canned artichoke hearts, drained
4 ounces thin green beans, cut into thirds	1 ¾ cups canned tomatoes, mashed
1-2 tablespoons vegetable oil	Salt
1 large onion, chopped	Pepper
1-2 cloves garlic, chopped	Chopped fresh parsley
3 cups sliced mushrooms	

Soak beans overnight in water. Cook according to package directions until tender; drain and set aside. Cook green beans in boiling water to cover until tender; set aside. Heat oil in a large skillet over medium-high heat. Add onion and garlic; sauté until onions are translucent. Add mushrooms and sauté 1 to 2 minutes. Combine kidney beans, green beans, onion mixture, artichoke hearts and tomatoes in a large bowl, blending well. Season to taste with salt and pepper. Spoon into a lightly greased 2-quart casserole dish; cover with foil. Bake at 350 degrees for 30 to 40 minutes. Sprinkle with parsley.

Yield: 4 to 6 servings

Shell and Dried Beans—You don't have to worry about protein when you eat beans. Combined with grain or dairy products, cooked dried beans provide a complete protein.

VEGETABLES & SIDE DISHES

Wild Rice with Snow Peas and Mushrooms

1 cup wild rice	2⅔ cups beef broth
5 tablespoons unsalted butter, divided	3½ ounces mushrooms, stems removed and cut into ¼-inch wide strips
¼ cup chopped carrot	⅓ pound snow peas, sliced diagonally into thirds
¼ cup chopped onion	Salt
¼ cup chopped celery	
⅓ cup white rice	
1 teaspoon dried tarragon	

Bring water to a boil in a large saucepan over high heat; stir in wild rice. Reduce heat and simmer for 15 minutes; drain. Melt 3 tablespoons butter in a large Dutch oven or soup pot over medium-high heat. Add carrot, onion and celery. Sauté for 4 minutes, stirring frequently. Stir in wild rice, white rice and tarragon, mixing well. Stir in broth. Bring mixture to a boil; reduce heat, and simmer for 40 minutes until all liquid is absorbed. Melt remaining 2 tablespoons butter in a skillet over medium-high heat. Add mushrooms and sauté 3 minutes. Add snow peas and sauté 1 minute or until crisp-tender. Stir mushrooms and snow peas into rice. Season to taste with salt.

Yield: 6 servings

Green pepper may change the flavor in frozen casseroles. Clove, garlic and pepper flavors get stronger when they are frozen, while sage, onion, and salt get milder or fade out.

Turkey Dressing Carlotta

6	slices bacon	1	cup chicken broth
1	cup chopped onion	2	large eggs, lightly beaten
1	cup chopped celery	1 ½	teaspoons salt
1	cup sliced mushroom	½	teaspoon poultry seasoning
4	cups fresh bread cubes	½	teaspoon dried sage
1	cup cranberries	½	teaspoon dried thyme
1	cup pecan meal or finely chopped pecans	½	teaspoon pepper

Cook bacon in a large skillet over medium-high heat until crisp. Remove bacon, reserving 1 tablespoon drippings in skillet; crumble and set aside. Heat drippings over medium-high heat. Add onion, celery and mushrooms; sauté until tender. Spoon vegetables into a large bowl. Stir in bacon, bread cubes, cranberries, pecan meal, broth, eggs, salt, poultry seasoning, sage, thyme and pepper. Add additional broth, if necessary, to hold mixture together. Spoon mixture into 1 large or 2 medium well greased baking pans; cover with foil.

Bake at 350 degrees for 20 minutes. Remove foil and bake 10 minutes. This recipe may also be used to stuff a 10 to 12-pound turkey.

Yield: 6 to 8 servings

 Eggplant—When cooked in combination with cheese, or served along with other high protein grains or vegetables, eggplant can form the basis for a very satisfying vegetarian meal.

VEGETABLES & SIDE DISHES

 # Hot Curried Fruit

"Wonderful for a brunch."

1 (16-ounce) can pear halves, drained well	1 (16-ounce) can apricot halves, drained well
1 (16-ounce) can peach halves, drained well	½ cup butter
1 (16-ounce) can pineapple chunks, drained well	¾ cup firmly packed light brown sugar
1 (16-ounce) can pitted Royal Anne cherries, drained well	3 tablespoons cornstarch
	1 ½ teaspoons curry powder

Arrange fruit in a shallow baking dish; set aside. Melt butter in a saucepan over medium heat. Stir in sugar, cornstarch and curry. Pour mixture over fruit. Cover and refrigerate 24 hours. Bake at 250 degrees for 1 hour. Serve hot.

Yield: 12 servings

 # Festive Fruit Compote

This recipe disappeared in no time flat at a recent Bargain Box picnic.

1 (8-ounce) package mixed dried fruits	⅓ cup firmly packed light brown sugar
1 (16-ounce) can cherry pie filling	½ teaspoon ground cinnamon
1 (11-ounce) can mandarin orange segments, drained	½ teaspoon nutmeg
	½ cup bourbon or apple juice

Combine dried fruits, pie filling and oranges in a bowl, tossing gently to blend. Spoon into a lightly greased 1 ½-quart casserole dish. Combine brown sugar, cinnamon, nutmeg and bourbon in a small bowl, stirring until sugar dissolves. Pour over fruit mixture; cover with foil. Bake at 350 degrees for 45 minutes. Serve warm.

Yield: 8 to 10 servings

HOW TO
PRESERVE A HUSBAND

From an 1871 Cook Book

Be careful in your selection. Do not choose one too young and take only such varieties as have been reared in a good atmosphere. When once decided upon and selected, let the part remain forever settled.

Some insist on keeping them in a pickle, while others are constantly getting into hot water.

This only makes them sour and bitter.

Even poor varieties may be made sweet, good and tender by garnishing with patience, well sweetened with smiles.

Wrap in a mantle of charity; keep warm with a steady fire of domestic devotion.

When thus prepared, husbands will keep for years and improve with age.

Sweet Endings

We prefer sweet endings to each day . . . don't you? From toothsome *Ambrosia* or succulent *Syllabub,* very old luscious Low Country desserts served after supper to distinguished guests, to a modern craving for rich creamy chocolate, you'll find deliciously delectable desserts in *Sweet Endings.*

Exquisite sparkling waters of the Atlantic Ocean lap against the winding white strand of Singleton's Beach. Silhouetted by the sun is an ancient Live Oak tree with wide-spread limbs windswept by ocean breezes and salt spray.

Sweetgrass seen in the foreground is used in local baskets for its pleasant hay-like fragrance. A traditional Low Country art form, it was brought to the Sea Islands by slaves from West Africa and has been passed down from generation to generation of Islanders. In use since the 18th century, Low Country coil basketry is one of the oldest local crafts. The baskets can be fashioned of marsh grasses, long leaf pine needles, bulrush or palmetto leaves. During rice and cotton cultivation, large coil baskets were made of bulrushes by men and used to collect and store vegetables, staples, fish, grain, cotton and for winnowing of rice. The most familiar baskets, made by women, are of soft pliable Sweetgrass—light in color when dry—and long leaf pine needles, a dark reddish rust color. A basket's value increases with age, and with proper care can last indefinitely. Sweetgrass baskets were used in homes for sewing notions, food and clothes storage, and are handy today as a centerpiece, or to serve cookies, brownies and other *Sweet Endings* to a lovely Low Country day.

Sweet Endings

Sweet Endings

SWEET ENDINGS

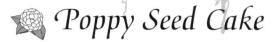 *Poppy Seed Cake*

⅓ cup poppy seeds
1 (18 ½-ounce) package white
cake mix

Lime-Butter Cream Frosting

Soak poppy seeds for 1 hour in total amount of liquid required by cake mix directions. Substitute this poppy seed mixture for milk or water in directions. Pour batter into 2 greased and floured 8-inch round cake pans or 1 greased and floured 13 x 9 x 2-inch baking pan. Bake according to package directions. Cool on a wire rack. Frost cake with Lime-Butter Cream Frosting.

Yield: 10 to 12 servings

Lime-Butter Cream Frosting:

½ cup butter
1 (16-ounce) box powdered
sugar
¼ teaspoon salt
1 egg white

1 teaspoon vanilla extract
1 ½ teaspoons grated lime peel
1 ½ tablespoons lime juice
Green food coloring

Cream butter in mixing bowl. Combine sugar and salt; add to butter mixture alternately with egg white. Beat until light and fluffy. Stir in vanilla, lime peel and lime juice. Stir in enough food coloring to tint frosting a pale green color.

 Grating orange or lemon rind is easier if the fruit is at room temperature.

SWEET ENDINGS

 # Harvest Apple Crisp

4	cups peeled and sliced apples (Jonathan or Granny Smith)	2	tablespoons water, if apples are not juicy
1	teaspoon ground cinnamon or nutmeg	1	cup sugar
		¾	cup all-purpose flour
		½	cup butter

Place apples in a lightly greased 8 x 8-inch baking dish. Sprinkle with cinnamon and add water, if necessary. Combine sugar and flour, mixing well. Cut in butter with a pastry blender or fork until crumbly. Sprinkle on apples, pressing down firmly. Bake at 350 degrees for 40 to 50 minutes until apples are tender. Serve warm with ice cream or whipped cream.

Yield: 6 to 8 servings

Layered Peach Dessert

¼	cup sugar	1	(8-ounce) package cream cheese, softened
3	cups chopped fresh peaches		
1 ½	cups all-purpose flour	1 ¾	cups sifted powdered sugar
¼	cup firmly packed light brown sugar	1	(8-ounce) container frozen whipped topping, thawed
½	cup chopped pecans	½	teaspoon almond extract
½	cup butter or margarine, melted		

Sprinkle sugar over peaches; stir gently and let stand 30 minutes. Combine flour, brown sugar and pecans in a medium bowl; stir in butter. Press into the bottom of a 13 x 9 x 2-inch baking dish. Bake at 350 degrees for 18 to 20 minutes. Cool crust on a wire rack. Combine cream cheese and powdered sugar in a mixing bowl; beat at medium speed until fluffy. Fold in whipped topping and almond extract. Drain peaches, discarding liquid. Fold peaches into cream cheese mixture. Spoon into crust, spreading evenly. Cover and refrigerate 3 to 4 hours.

Yield: 10 to 12 servings

SWEET ENDINGS

Frozen Strawberry Cake

1   cup cookie or graham cracker crumbs
2   tablespoons melted butter or margarine
1   (10-ounce) package frozen strawberries, thawed
2   egg whites
½   cup sugar
1   cup heavy whipping cream, whipped

Combine crumbs and butter in a small bowl, blending well. Sprinkle in the bottom of a 9-inch springform pan; set aside. Beat strawberries, egg whites and sugar at medium speed with an electric mixer for 15 minutes. Fold in whipped cream. Spoon mixture over crust. Cover with plastic wrap and freeze 8 hours or overnight. (Recipe will keep in the freezer a long time.) Remove sides of springform pan; serve frozen.

Yield: 8 to 12 servings

Note: egg whites need to be at room temperature for greater volume when whipped.

Figs in Red Wine and Cream

2   cups sweet red wine
3   tablespoons honey
1   pound dried Calimyrna figs, whole or quartered
1   cup heavy whipping cream
    Ground cinnamon

Combine wine and honey in a saucepan. Bring to a boil; stir in figs. Reduce heat, and simmer for 1 hour. Remove from heat; let cool. Do not drain. Beat whipping cream at medium-high speed with an electric mixer until soft peaks form. Fold into fig mixture. Serve in a large pottery or ceramic bowl; sprinkle with cinnamon.

Yield: 6 to 8 servings

Bread Pudding with Raspberry Sauce

Here's a new twist on an old-fashioned favorite.

12	thin slices French bread	4	cups milk
	Butter	1	cup heavy whipping cream
5	large eggs	1	teaspoon vanilla extract
4	egg yolks		Sifted powdered sugar
1	cup sugar		Raspberry jelly
⅛	teaspoon salt		

Remove crusts from bread and spread butter on one side. Place the bread, butter side up, in a lightly greased 2-quart baking dish. Beat eggs, yolks, sugar and salt until well blended. Stir in milk, cream and vanilla. Pour mixture over the bread. Place the baking dish in a second larger baking dish or roasting pan; pour hot water to the depth of 1 inch. Bake at 375 degrees for 45 minutes or until a knife inserted in the center comes out clean. Sprinkle with powdered sugar; run pan under a broiler to glaze pudding, watching carefully to avoid burning. Thin raspberry jelly with enough water to make a pourable consistency. Serve sauce over each serving.

Yield: 6 to 8 servings

Lemon Curd

2	lemons	3	large eggs, lightly beaten
1	cup sugar	6	tablespoons butter

Peel lemons thinly, taking care not to include the bitter white pith. Cut lemons in half and squeeze juice into a non-reactive (enamel or stainless steel) saucepan. Add lemon peel, sugar and eggs. Cook over low heat, stirring constantly, until thickened. (Do not boil.) Add butter, stirring until butter melts. Remove from heat; strain lemon peel and pour into jars. Seal jars and store in refrigerator. Serve with scones.

Yield: 1 pint

Mocha Pudding Cake

1	cup all-purpose flour	1 ½	tablespoons instant coffee
2	teaspoons baking powder		granules
¼	teaspoon salt	½	cup low-fat milk
1	cup sugar, divided	3	tablespoons vegetable oil
¼	cup plus 2 tablespoons	1	teaspoon vanilla extract
	cocoa, divided	1	cup boiling water

Combine flour, baking powder, salt, ⅔ cup sugar, ¼ cup cocoa and coffee in a large bowl. Combine milk, oil and vanilla; stir into dry ingredients. Spoon mixture into an 8 x 8-inch baking pan coated with vegetable cooking spray. Combine remaining ⅓ cup sugar and 2 tablespoons cocoa; sprinkle over batter. Pour boiling water over batter (do not stir). Bake at 350 degrees for 30 minutes until cake springs back when lightly touched. Serve warm with ice cream.

Yield: 9 servings

 # Sautéed Bananas in Rum

8	firm, ripe bananas, peeled and	2	tablespoons dark rum or
	cut into 1-inch pieces		apple juice
½	honey, sugar or brown sugar		Grated peel of 1 orange
1	teaspoon unsalted butter	1	cup orange juice
		1	cup low-fat vanilla yogurt

Heat bananas, honey and butter in a skillet over medium heat, stirring until butter has melted. Add rum, stirring until thoroughly heated. Ignite sauce carefully with a grill lighter or long fireplace match. Cook 1 minute, shaking pan, until flames subside. Add orange rind and juice; cook for 10 minutes, stirring often, until bananas are tender. To serve, drizzle yogurt over hot bananas, or serve with ice cream.

Yield: 8 servings

SWEET ENDINGS

Carolina Peach Cobbler

2	cups sliced peaches	2	teaspoons baking powder
1 ½	cups sugar, divided	¼	teaspoon salt
½	cup butter or margarine	¾	cup milk
¾	cup all-purpose flour		

Combine peaches and ½ cup sugar in a bowl, tossing to coat; set aside. Place butter in the bottom of a 2-quart baking dish; place in a 350 degree oven to melt. Combine remaining 1 cup sugar, flour, baking powder, and salt in a bowl, stirring well. Stir in milk. Spoon batter over the melted butter; do not stir. Spoon peaches over batter; do not stir. Bake at 350 degrees for 35 to 45 minutes until light brown, crisp and puffy. Blueberries may be substituted for peaches. Use frozen fruit only if fresh fruit is not available.

Yield: 8 servings

 # Low Country Lemon Syllabub

1	lemon	3	tablespoons brandy
3	tablespoons sugar	3	tablespoons sherry
1	cup heavy whipping cream		

Peel lemon thinly, taking care not to include the bitter white pith. Place peel in a small bowl. Cut lemon in half and squeeze juice into bowl. Let the peel soak in the juice for a few hours. Strain the lemon juice into sugar in a mixing bowl. Stir in cream, brandy and sherry. Beat at high speed with an electric mixer until soft peaks form. Spoon into individual serving glasses and refrigerate 8 hours or overnight.

Yield: 4 to 6 servings

SWEET ENDINGS

Brandied Caramel Flan

1 ¼	cups sugar, divided	½	teaspoon salt
2	cups milk	2	teaspoons vanilla extract
2	cups heavy whipping cream	⅓	cup brandy or Kahlúa
6	large eggs		

Place an 8-inch round shallow baking dish in a 350 degree oven to heat. Place ¾ cup sugar in a heavy skillet over medium heat. Cook 10 to 15 minutes until sugar melts and forms a light brown syrup. Do not stir sugar until it begins to brown; then stir to blend. Immediately pour caramelized sugar into the heated baking dish. Holding dish with a potholder, rotate dish to cover bottom and sides with sugar mixture. The dish must be hot and you must work quickly. Combine milk and cream in a saucepan over medium heat; cook until bubbles form around edges of pan. Combine eggs, remaining ½ cup sugar, salt, and vanilla in a large mixing bowl; beat at medium speed with an electric mixer until well blended. Gradually add hot milk mixture and brandy. Pour into prepared dish. Place the custard dish in a second larger baking dish or roasting pan; pour hot water to the depth of 1 inch. Bake at 350 degrees for 1 hour or until a knife inserted in the center comes out clean. Let custard cool, then cover and refrigerate 4 hours or overnight. Loosen edges with a knife and invert on a serving plate.

Yield: 8 servings

SWEET ENDINGS

🍃 John Jakes' Butter Fudge Fingers

This recipe has been in our family since the 1950's. Back then, with kids growing up and sugar of no concern, we consumed a couple of pans a week. Where the recipe originated, I don't know or can't remember (probably the latter!). I do know these goodies are deliciously addictive (as the slogan for some food or other says, you can't eat just one), and seriously damaging to the waistline. We love Butter Fudge Fingers anyway, make them for friends at Christmas, and never found another treat to match them.

2	(1-ounce) squares unsweetened chocolate, melted	2	large eggs
		¾	cup all-purpose flour
⅓	cup butter, melted	½	teaspoon baking powder
1	cup sugar	½	teaspoon salt
		½	cup chopped nuts

Topping:

¼	cup butter	1	(1-ounce) square unsweetened chocolate, melted
2	cups sifted powdered sugar		
2	tablespoons heavy whipping cream	1	tablespoon butter, melted
1	tablespoon vanilla extract		

Combine chocolate and butter in a mixing bowl; beat in sugar and eggs. Combine flour, baking powder and salt; stir into chocolate mixture. Fold in nuts. Spread batter in a lightly greased 8 x 8-inch baking pan. Bake at 350 degrees for 30 minutes. Cool completely on a wire rack. Melt butter; add powdered sugar, stirring until well blended. Stir in cream and vanilla. Spread mixture over cooled brownies. Combine chocolate and 1 tablespoon melted butter; drizzle mixture over topping. Let cool. Cut into 2 x 1-inch bars.

Yield: 32 pieces

Since we came to Hilton Head more than 22 years ago, we have continually seen the wonderful and useful work done by The Bargain Box, and their generous support of other community organizations. I can do no less than take part in your newest undertaking! - and thank you for asking.

John Jakes is an author and playwright of international acclaim and an ardent supporter of the Low Country art community and charitable agencies.

Amaretto Mousse Cheesecake

2	cups graham cracker crumbs	1	(5-ounce) can evaporated milk
½	cup butter or margarine, melted	1	teaspoon lemon juice
1	(¼-ounce) envelope unflavored gelatin	⅓	cup almond-flavored liqueur
½	cup cold water	1	teaspoon vanilla extract
3	(8-ounce) packages cream cheese, softened	¾	cup heavy whipping cream, whipped
1 ¼	cups sugar		Garnishes: shaved chocolate or chocolate sauce

Combine graham cracker crumbs and butter in a small bowl, mixing well. Press into the bottom and up the sides of a 9-inch springform pan; refrigerate until chilled. Sprinkle gelatin over cold water in a small saucepan; let stand 1 minute. Stir over low heat for 3 minutes or until completely dissolved; set aside. Beat cream cheese and sugar at medium speed with an electric mixer about 2 minutes or until fluffy. Gradually add evaporated milk and lemon juice; beat at medium-high speed about 2 minutes until very fluffy. Gradually beat in gelatin mixture, liqueur, and vanilla. Fold in whipped cream. Pour mixture into crust. Cover and refrigerate 8 hours or overnight. Remove sides of pan and garnish with shaved chocolate or chocolate sauce.

Yield: 12 to 16 servings

SWEET ENDINGS

 *Overnight Delight Cookies*

3 egg whites	1 cup sugar
Pinch salt	1 cup mini chocolate morsels
¼ teaspoon ground cinnamon	1 cup chopped nuts

Preheat oven to 350 degrees. Beat egg whites (at room temperature) at high speed with an electric mixer until foamy. Stir in salt and cinnamon. Gradually add sugar, 1 tablespoon at a time, beating until stiff peaks form. Fold in morsels and nuts. Drop by teaspoonfuls onto greased baking sheets. Place in preheated oven and immediately turn off heat. Do not open oven door for at least 8 hours. Remove from oven and store in an airtight container.

Yield: 2 dozen

Mother's Peanut Bars

"A child's delight."

1 cup all-purpose flour	⅓ cup hot water
1 cup sifted powdered sugar	Powdered Sugar Icing
1 teaspoon baking powder	Finely ground salted peanuts
2 large eggs	

Beat flour, sugar, baking powder, eggs and hot water together in a mixing bowl until forming a smooth batter. Spoon into a greased 13 x 9 x 2-inch baking pan. Bake at 350 degrees for 15 to 20 minutes. Cool completely on a wire rack. Cut into bars. Frost bars on all sides with a thin layer of Powdered Sugar Icing and roll in peanuts.

Powdered Sugar Icing:

2 cups sifted powdered sugar	¼ cup milk

Beat together sugar and milk until smooth and spreadable.

Yield: about 30 bars

🌿 *Melting Moments*

A cream cheese or lemon frosting adds flavor.

1 cup butter, softened	½ teaspoon almond extract
2 tablespoons sifted powdered sugar	2 cups sifted cake flour
	Prepared butter frosting

Beat butter at medium speed with an electric mixer until creamy; gradually add sugar and extract, beating well. Add flour, beating at low speed until blended. Drop by teaspoonfuls onto ungreased baking sheets. Bake at 325 degrees for 15 minutes. Remove cookies to wire racks; cool completely. Put cookies together with butter frosting to resemble tiny cookie sandwiches.

Yield: 2½ dozen

Snappy Sugar Crisps 🌿

1 cup butter, melted	3 cups all-purpose flour
1½ cups sugar	1 teaspoon salt
2 large eggs	½ teaspoon baking powder
2 teaspoons vanilla extract	

Combine butter, sugar, eggs and vanilla in a mixing bowl; beat at medium-high speed with an electric mixer until light and fluffy. Combine flour, salt and baking powder; stir into butter mixture. Wrap dough in plastic wrap and refrigerate at least 1 hour or overnight. Roll dough to ⅛-inch thickness on a lightly floured surface. Cut with cookie cutter and place on an ungreased baking sheet. Bake at 350 degrees for 10 minutes.

Yield: 3 to 4 dozen

Note: dough can be formed into a roll, refrigerated or frozen and cut into slices before baking.

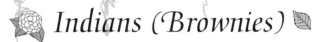 Indians (Brownies)

1 cup butter or margarine	2 teaspoons vanilla extract
4 (1-ounce) squares unsweetened chocolate	1 cup all-purpose flour
	2 teaspoons baking powder
2 cups sugar	2 cups chopped nuts
4 large eggs, lightly beaten	

Melt butter and chocolate in a heavy saucepan over low heat. Stir in sugar, eggs, vanilla, flour, baking powder and nuts, blending well. Spread batter into a lightly greased 13 x 9 x 2-inch baking pan. Bake at 350 degrees for 30 minutes. Cool completely on a wire rack and cut into bars.

Yield: 2 to 2½ dozen

Layered Fudge Bars

½ cup shortening	¾ teaspoon salt, divided
1 cup firmly packed light brown sugar	2 cups quick oats
	1 (6-ounce) package semisweet chocolate morsels
1 large egg	1 tablespoon butter
1½ teaspoons vanilla extract, divided	1 cup sweetened condensed milk
¾ cup all-purpose flour	½ cup chopped nuts
½ teaspoon baking soda	

Cream shortening; gradually add brown sugar, beating well at medium speed with an electric mixer. Add egg and ½ teaspoon vanilla; beat well. Combine flour, soda and ¼ teaspoon salt; add to creamed mixture, mixing well. Stir in oats; set aside 1 cup. Press remaining oat mixture in the bottom of an 11 x 7 x 1½-inch baking pan. Combine morsels, butter, condensed milk and remaining ½ teaspoon salt in top of a double boiler. Bring water to a boil. Reduce heat to low; cook, stirring constantly, until chocolate melts. Stir in remaining 1 teaspoon vanilla and nuts. Spread chocolate mixture over oat layer; sprinkle with reserved oat mixture. Bake at 350 degrees for 25 minutes.

Yield: 15 to 18 bars

SWEET ENDINGS

Ginger Snaps

2	cups all-purpose flour	½	teaspoon salt
1	cup sugar	½	teaspoon ground cloves
1	teaspoon baking soda	¾	cup shortening
1	teaspoon ground cinnamon	¼	cup molasses
1	teaspoon ground ginger	1	large egg, lightly beaten

Combine flour, sugar, baking soda, cinnamon, ginger, salt and cloves in a large bowl, mix well. Cut in shortening with a pastry blender or fork until mixture is crumbly. Stir in molasses and egg. Shape dough into 1-inch balls; roll in sugar and place on ungreased baking sheets. Flatten slightly. Bake at 350 degrees for 10 minutes.

Yield: 3 dozen

The World's Best Cookies

1	cup butter	½	cup shredded coconut
1	cup sugar	1	cup oats
1	cup firmly packed lightly brown sugar	1	cup crushed cornflake cereal
		½	cup chopped pecans
1	large egg	3 ½	cups all-purpose flour
1	cup canola oil	1	teaspoon baking soda
2	teaspoons vanilla extract	1	teaspoon salt

Cream butter; gradually add sugars, beating well at medium speed with an electric mixer. Add egg, oil and vanilla; beat well. Stir in coconut, oats, crushed cereal and pecans. Combine flour, soda and salt; add to creamed mixture, mixing well. Roll dough into marble-sized balls, then flatten each with the tines of a fork; place on ungreased baking sheets 2 inches apart (cookies will spread). Bake at 350 degrees for 12 minutes. Cool on wire racks. Store in an airtight container.

Yield: 4 dozen

Jumbles

½ cup butter or margarine
1 cup firmly packed light brown
   sugar
2 large eggs
1 teaspoon vanilla extract
1 ⅞ cups all-purpose flour

1 teaspoon baking soda
   Dash salt
1 cup flaked coconut
1 cup chopped dates
¼ cup chopped cherries
1 cup chopped nuts

Cream butter; gradually add brown sugar, beating well at medium speed with an electric mixer. Add eggs, one at a time, beating well after each addition. Stir in vanilla. Combine flour, soda and salt; add to creamed mixture, mixing well. Stir in coconut, dates, cherries and nuts. Drop dough by teaspoonfuls onto greased baking sheets. Bake at 350 degrees for 10 to 12 minutes or until golden brown. Cookies freeze well. Dough may be prepared ahead and refrigerated until ready to bake.

Yield: 3 dozen

Chocolate Crinkles

½ cup shortening
1 ⅔ cups sugar
2 large eggs, lightly beaten
2 ounces unsweetened
   chocolate, melted
2 teaspoons vanilla extract

2 cups all-purpose flour
2 teaspoons baking powder
½ teaspoon salt
⅓ cup milk
½ cup chopped nuts
   Sifted powdered sugar

Cream butter; gradually add sugar, beating well at medium speed with an electric mixer. Add eggs, chocolate and vanilla; beat well. Combine flour, baking powder and salt; add to butter mixture, alternately with milk. Stir in nuts. Cover and refrigerate 2 to 3 hours. Shape dough into 1-inch balls and roll in powdered sugar; place on a greased baking sheet. Bake at 350 degrees for 15 minutes. Cool slightly before removing from baking sheet.

Yield: 4 dozen

Turtle Bars

2 cups all-purpose flour	½ cup butter
1 cup firmly packed light brown sugar	1 ½ cups pecan halves

Topping:

⅔ cup butter	1 (11 ½-ounce) bag milk chocolate morsels
½ cup firmly packed light brown sugar	

Combine flour and 1 cup brown sugar in a large bowl, mixing well. Cut in ½ cup butter with a pastry blender or fork until mixture resembles coarse crumbs. Press into an ungreased 15 x 10-inch jelly-roll pan. Sprinkle pecans evenly over top. Combine remaining ⅔ cup butter and ½ cup brown sugar in a saucepan over medium heat, stirring constantly until mixture begins to boil. Boil for 1 minute and pour over pecans. Bake at 350 degrees for 20 to 25 minutes or until firm. Remove from the oven immediately and sprinkle with chocolate morsels, spreading to cover. Cool completely on a wire rack and cut into squares.

Yield: 3 dozen

*No matter where I take my guests,
they seem to like my kitchen best.*

Crème De Menthe Squares

1 ¼ cups butter, divided
½ cup cocoa powder
3 ½ cups sifted powdered sugar, divided
1 large egg

1 teaspoon vanilla extract
2 cups graham cracker crumbs
⅓ cup crème de menthe
1 ½ cups semisweet chocolate morsels

Combine ½ cup butter and cocoa in a saucepan over medium heat; cook, stirring constantly, until well blended. Remove from heat and add ½ cup powdered sugar, egg and vanilla. Stir in graham cracker crumbs, mixing well. Press into the bottom of an ungreased 13 x 9 x 2-inch baking pan. Melt ½ cup butter. Combine melted butter and liqueur in a mixing bowl. Beat in the remaining 3 cups of powdered sugar until smooth. Spread over chocolate layer. Refrigerate for 1 hour. Combine remaining ¼ cup butter and chocolate morsels in a small saucepan. Cook over low heat, stirring constantly, until mixture is smooth. Spread over the mint layer. Refrigerate until firm; cut into squares. Cover and refrigerate until ready to serve.

Yield: 6 to 7 dozen

Cheese Cake Squares

1 (18 ½-ounce) box yellow cake mix with pudding
½ cup butter or margarine, melted
4 large eggs, divided

1 (8-ounce) package cream cheese, softened
1 (16-ounce) box powdered sugar

Combine cake mix, butter and 1 egg in a large bowl. Beat together until well blended. Press into a greased 13 x 9 x 2-inch baking pan. Combine cream cheese, sugar and remaining 3 eggs in a large bowl. Beat together until well blended. Pour mixture over crust. Bake at 350 degrees for 35 minutes. Cool on a wire rack. Cut into bars.

Yield: 2 to 2 ½ dozen

SWEET ENDINGS

 *Snippy Doodles*

During a busy day of baking, I mistakenly doubled the baking powder and used nutmeg instead of cinnamon. The result made for a great variation of these easy-to-do bars.

2	tablespoons shortening	1	teaspoon baking powder
⅔	cup sugar	1	teaspoon ground cinnamon
1	large egg	½	teaspoon salt
1	cup sifted cake flour	½	cup milk

Cream shortening; gradually add sugar, beating well at medium speed with an electric mixer. Add egg, mixing well. Combine flour, baking powder, cinnamon and salt; add to creamed mixture alternately with milk. Spoon mixture into a greased 13 x 9 x 2-inch baking pan. Bake at 350 degrees for 15 minutes. Sprinkle with sugar and bake 10 minutes. Cool completely on a wire rack and cut into squares.

Yield: 2 dozen

Orange Cookies

These are good lunch-box cookies.

2	cups butter or margarine	¼	cup frozen orange juice concentrate, thawed
1	cup sugar		
1	cup firmly packed light brown sugar	6	cups all-purpose flour
		½	teaspoon baking soda
2	large eggs	½	teaspoon salt
1	teaspoon vanilla extract		

Cream butter; gradually add sugars, beating well at medium speed with an electric mixer. Add eggs, one at a time, beating well after each addition. Stir in vanilla and orange juice concentrate. Combine flour, soda and salt; add to creamed mixture, mixing well. Drop by teaspoonfuls onto ungreased baking sheets. Bake at 375 degrees for about 8 minutes. Cool on a wire rack.

Yield: 6 dozen

Almond Joy Bars

1 ½ cups graham cracker crumbs
1 ¼ cups sugar, divided
¾ cup butter, melted, divided
1 (15-ounce) can sweetened condensed milk
1 (8-ounce) package flaked coconut
⅓ cup milk
3 tablespoons cocoa
1 teaspoon vanilla extract

Combine crumbs, ¼ cup sugar and ½ cup melted butter in a bowl; press into the bottom of a 9 x 9-inch baking pan. Combine condensed milk and coconut; spread over graham cracker crust. Bake at 325 degrees for 30 minutes; cool on a wire rack. Combine remaining 1 cup sugar, remaining ¼ cup melted butter, milk and cocoa in a saucepan over medium-high heat. Bring to a boil; boil 5 minutes. Stir in vanilla. Beat with a wooden spoon or electric mixer until thick enough to spread. Spread chocolate mixture over coconut; refrigerate until firm. Cut into squares.

Yield: 2 to 2 ½ dozen

Chocolate Mint Cookies

¾ cup butter or margarine
1 ½ cups firmly packed light brown sugar
2 tablespoons water
1 (12-ounce) package semisweet chocolate morsels
2 large eggs
2 ½ cups all-purpose flour
1 ¼ teaspoons baking soda
½ teaspoon salt
1 (16-ounce) package layered green chocolate mints

Heat butter, sugar and water in a large saucepan over low heat, stirring until butter melts. Add chocolate morsels and stir until partially melted. Remove from heat and continue to stir until all chocolate is melted. Pour into a large bowl; cool for 10 minutes. Add eggs, one at a time, beating well after each addition. Combine flour, baking soda and salt; beat into chocolate mixture at low speed until blended. Cover and refrigerate for 1 hour. Roll into 1-inch balls and place, 2 inches apart, on foil-lined baking sheets. Bake at 350 degrees for 12 minutes. Place a mint on each cookie and spread as it melts. Remove from pan and cool on a wire rack.

Yield: 3 dozen

Choco-Peanut Cookies

½ cup shortening
½ cup sugar
2 ounces unsweetened chocolate, melted, divided
1 large egg
1 teaspoon vanilla extract
1 cup plus 3 tablespoons all-purpose flour, divided

½ teaspoon soda
1 teaspoon salt
½ cup firmly packed light brown sugar
¼ cup peanut butter
2 tablespoons melted butter

Cream shortening; gradually add sugar, beating well at medium speed with an electric mixer. Add chocolate, egg and vanilla; beat well. Combine 1 cup flour, soda and salt; add to creamed mixture, mixing well. Combine remaining 3 tablespoons flour, brown sugar, peanut butter and melted butter, beating until well blended. Drop chocolate mixture by teaspoonfuls 1 inch apart onto greased baking sheets. Top each with ½ teaspoon of peanut butter dough. Dip fork in flour and press down gently. Bake at 325 degrees for 12 minutes. Cool on a wire rack. Cut into bars.

Yield: about 4 dozen

 Tin coffee cans make excellent freezer containers for cookies.

Stuffed Date Drops

12 pecan or walnut halves	¾ cup all-purpose flour
24 pitted whole dates	¼ teaspoon baking powder
2 tablespoons shortening	¼ teaspoon baking soda
½ cup firmly packed light brown sugar	½ cup sour cream
	Golden Frosting
1 egg yolk	

Slice pecan halves lengthwise into 2 pieces. Stuff dates with nuts; set aside. Cream shortening; gradually add sugar, beating well at medium speed with an electric mixer. Add egg yolk, mixing well. Combine flour, baking powder and baking soda; add to shortening mixture alternately with sour cream. Stir in stuffed dates. Drop dough by rounded teaspoonfuls, with 1 date per cookie onto a greased baking sheet. Bake at 375 degrees 7 to 9 minutes or until golden. Cool on wire rack; frost with Golden Frosting.

Yield: 2 dozen

Golden Frosting:

2 tablespoons butter or margarine	⅛ teaspoon vanilla extract
¾ cup sifted powdered sugar	Milk

Heat butter in a medium saucepan over medium-low heat for 10 minutes or until light brown. Remove from heat. Gradually stir in powdered sugar and vanilla (mixture will be crumbly). Gradually stir in enough milk to bring mixture to a spreadable consistency.

Yield: about ⅓ cup

Big, Soft Ginger Cookies

These cookies soften more a day after baking.
They have a wonderful spicy aroma and taste.

¾ cup butter, margarine or
    shortening
1 cup sugar
1 large egg
¼ cup molasses
2 ¼ cups all-purpose flour

1 teaspoon ground ginger
1 teaspoon baking soda
¾ teaspoon ground cinnamon
½ teaspoon ground cloves
    Sugar

Cream butter; gradually add sugar, beating well at medium speed with an electric mixer. Add egg and molasses, mixing well. Combine flour, ginger, baking soda, cinnamon and cloves; add to creamed mixture, mixing well. Shape dough into 1 ½-inch balls (about 1 heaping tablespoon). Roll in sugar and place, 2 ½ inches apart, on ungreased baking sheets. Bake at 350 degrees for 10 minutes or until light brown and still puffed (do not overbake). Let stand for 2 minutes; transfer to a wire rack to cool.

Yield: 2 dozen, 3-inch cookies

SWEET ENDINGS

🍃 Chocolate Chip Oatmeal Cookies

*These cookies freeze well and are
a big favorite with children (of all ages!).*

1	cup butter or shortening	2	cup quick-cooking oats
¾	cup sugar	1 ½	cups all-purpose flour
¾	cup firmly packed light brown sugar	1	teaspoon baking soda
		1	teaspoon salt
2	large eggs	1	(6-ounce) package semisweet chocolate morsels
1	teaspoon hot water		
1	teaspoon vanilla extract	1	cup nuts, coarsely chopped

Cream butter; gradually add sugars, beating well at medium speed with an electric mixer. Add eggs, hot water and vanilla, mixing well. Combine oats, flour, baking soda and salt; add to creamed mixture, mixing well. Stir in chocolate morsels and nuts. Drop dough by teaspoonfuls onto greased baking sheets. Bake at 375 degrees for 10 to 12 minutes. Remove from pan and cool on a wire rack.

Yield: 3 dozen

Note: raisins may be substituted for the chocolate morsels, or use half raisins and half chocolate morsels.

Super Rum Cake ✓

1 cup chopped pecans or walnuts	¾ cup water, divided
1 (18 ½-ounce) package yellow cake mix with pudding	⅓ cup vegetable oil
	1 cup dark rum, divided
3 large eggs	½ cup butter
	1 cup sugar

Grease and flour a 10-inch tube or 12-cup Bundt pan. Sprinkle nuts in bottom of pan; set aside. Combine cake mix, eggs, ½ cup water, oil and ½ cup rum in a mixing bowl. Beat at medium speed until well blended. Pour batter over nuts. Bake at 325 degrees for 1 hour. Cool; invert pan onto a serving plate. Heat butter in a saucepan over medium heat; stir in remaining ¼ cup water and sugar. Bring mixture to a boil; boil 5 minutes, stirring constantly. Remove from heat and stir in remaining ½ cup rum. Prick top of cake with a fork; pour glaze over the top and sides.

Note: A lemon cake mix with pudding may be substituted for a flavor variation.

Pecan Cake

½ cup butter	1 teaspoon vanilla extract
½ cup margarine	2 cups all-purpose flour
2 cups sugar	2 teaspoons baking powder
4 large eggs	¼ teaspoon salt
½ cup milk	1 cup finely chopped pecans

Beat butter and margarine at medium speed with an electric mixer; gradually add sugar, beating well. Add eggs, one at a time, beating well after each addition. Beat in milk and vanilla. Stir in flour, baking powder and salt. Beat at high speed for 20 minutes. Add nuts and beat until blended. Pour batter into a greased and floured tube pan. Put pan in a cold oven and set temperature to 350 degrees. Bake for 60 to 65 minutes. Cool on rack. Invert onto a serving plate.

Yield: 12 to 16 servings

Plum Cake

This recipe can be used as a breakfast or brunch bread.

2 cups all-purpose flour	3 large eggs, lightly beaten
1 ¾ cups sugar	2 (4 ½-ounce) jars plums with
1 teaspoon ground cinnamon	tapioca (baby food)
½ teaspoon baking soda	¼ teaspoon red food coloring
½ teaspoon ground cloves	1 cup chopped nuts
1 cup vegetable oil	Orange Spread

Combine flour, sugar, cinnamon, soda and cloves in a large mixing bowl. Stir in oil, eggs, plums and food coloring, mixing well. Stir in nuts. Pour into a greased 9 x 5 x 3-inch loaf pan. Bake at 350 degrees for 60 to 70 minutes. Cool in pan 10 minutes; remove from pan and let cool completely on a wire rack. Spread Orange Spread on top.

Orange Spread:

1 (8-ounce) package cream cheese, softened	3 tablespoons frozen orange juice concentrate, thawed
	Sugar or orange marmalade

Combine cream cheese and juice concentrate, stirring until well blended. Sweeten to taste with sugar or orange marmalade.

Yield: about 1 cup

SWEET ENDINGS

Great Depression Cake ✓

*Sift powdered sugar through a doily on
top of the cake for a more attractive presentation.*

2 cups sugar	1 teaspoon baking soda
2 cups strong brewed coffee	1 teaspoon ground cinnamon
½ cup shortening or margarine	1 teaspoon allspice
2 cups raisins	1 teaspoon ground cloves
1 apple, grated	1 teaspoon nutmeg
2 cups all-purpose flour	1 cup chopped nuts
2 teaspoons baking powder	

Combine sugar, coffee, shortening, raisins and apple in a large saucepan over medium-high heat. Bring to boil; reduce heat and simmer 10 minutes. Cool. Combine flour, baking powder, baking soda, cinnamon, allspice, cloves and nutmeg in a bowl; stir into cooled mixture, blending well. Stir in nuts. Pour into a greased and floured 13 x 9 x 2-inch baking pan. Bake at 350 degrees for 1 hour. Cool completely on a wire rack.

 # Pumpkin Cake

1 (28-ounce) can pumpkin	½ teaspoon nutmeg
1 ½ cups sugar	1 (18 ½-ounce) box yellow cake mix
4 large eggs	
1 (12-ounce) can evaporated milk	½ cup butter or margarine, melted
2 teaspoons ground cinnamon	1 cup chopped nuts
1 teaspoon ground ginger	

Combine pumpkin, sugar, eggs, milk, cinnamon, ginger and nutmeg in a large bowl; beat well at medium speed with an electric mixer until blended. Pour into an ungreased 13 x 9 x 2-inch baking pan. Sprinkle with yellow cake mix. Pour butter over cake mix and sprinkle with nuts. Bake at 350 degrees for 1 hour (do not overbake).

Yield: 12 servings

✓ *Old Kentucky Jam Cake*

½ (15-ounce) box raisins	1 teaspoon salt
¼ cup fruit juice	1 teaspoon baking soda
½ cup butter or shortening	1 teaspoon nutmeg
1 cup sugar	1 teaspoon ground cinnamon
3 large eggs, separated	1 teaspoon ground cloves
1 cup blackberry jam	½ cup buttermilk
2 cups all-purpose flour	Caramel Frosting

Combine raisins and juice in a small bowl; let stand until softened. Cream butter; gradually add sugar, beating well at medium speed with an electric mixer. Beat in egg yolks. Stir in jam. Combine flour, salt, baking soda, nutmeg, cinnamon and cloves; add to butter mixture alternately with buttermilk. Fold in raisin mixture. Beat egg whites (at room temperature) in a large bowl until soft peaks form. Gently fold egg whites into flour mixture. Pour into 2 greased and floured 8-inch round cake pans. Bake at 350 degrees for 40 to 60 minutes. Cool in pans 10 minutes; remove from pans, and let cool completely on wire racks. Spread Caramel Frosting between layers and on top and sides of cake.

Caramel Frosting:

½ cup butter or margarine	¼ cup milk
1 ½ cups firmly packed light brown sugar	1 teaspoon vanilla extract
	2 cups sifted powdered sugar

Melt butter in a large saucepan over medium-high heat; stir in sugar. Bring mixture to a boil, and add milk. Remove from heat and cool. Stir in vanilla and powdered sugar.

Tomato Soup Cake ✓

Taste testing this cake brought "rave reviews" from our volunteers.

¼	cup shortening	½	teaspoon ground cloves
1	cup sugar	1	(10 ¾-ounce) can tomato soup
2	cups all-purpose flour	½	can water
2	teaspoons baking powder	1	cup chopped walnuts
1	teaspoon baking soda	1	cup raisins
1	teaspoon ground cinnamon		Prepared cream cheese
1	teaspoon nutmeg		frosting (optional)

Cream shortening; gradually add sugar, beating well at medium speed with an electric mixer. Combine flour, baking powder, baking soda, cinnamon, nutmeg and cloves; add to shortening mixture alternately with tomato soup and water, beating well. Stir in nuts and raisins. Pour into a greased 8 x 4 x 3-inch loaf pan. Bake at 350 degrees for 60 to 70 minutes. Cool completely; let stand for 24 hours before cutting. Spread prepared cream cheese frosting over the top, if desired.

Apple Cake

¾	cup unsalted butter or margarine	¾	teaspoon salt (omit if using salted butter)
1 ½	cups sugar	¾	teaspoon ground cinnamon
2	large eggs	¾	teaspoon baking soda
1 ½	cups unbleached all-purpose flour	6	cups tart apples, peeled, cored and sliced
		¾	cup chopped walnuts

Cream butter; gradually add sugar, beating well at medium speed with an electric mixer. Add eggs, beating well. Combine flour, salt, cinnamon and baking soda; add to butter mixture, beating well. Stir in apples and nuts. Mixture will be thick. Spoon batter into a greased 9 x 9-inch baking pan. Bake at 350 degrees for 1 hour or until a toothpick inserted in the center comes out clean. Serve warm or at room temperature.

Yield: 9 servings

SWEET ENDINGS

Siren's Chocolate Cake

½ cup butter or margarine	2 ½ cups all-purpose flour
4 (1-ounce) squares unsweetened chocolate	2 cups sugar
	2 teaspoons baking soda
2 large eggs	½ teaspoon salt
2 cups buttermilk	Chocolate Frosting
2 teaspoons vanilla extract	

Melt butter and chocolate in a small saucepan over low heat; cool and set aside. Beat eggs at medium speed with an electric mixer; add buttermilk and vanilla. Combine flour, sugar, baking soda and salt; gradually add to egg mixture. Stir in chocolate mixture, blending well. Pour into 2 greased and floured 9-inch round cake pans. Bake at 350 degrees for 35 to 40 minutes or until a toothpick inserted in the center comes out clean. Cool in pans 10 minutes; remove from pans, and let cool completely on wire racks. Spread Chocolate Frosting between layers and on top and sides of cake.

Yield: 12 to 16 servings

Note: 2 cups milk with 3 tablespoons lemon juice may be substituted for buttermilk.

Chocolate Frosting:

½ cup butter or margarine	1 (16-ounce) box powdered sugar, sifted
4 (1-ounce) squares unsweetened chocolate	1 (5-ounce) can evaporated milk
	2 teaspoons vanilla extract

Melt butter and chocolate in a small saucepan over low heat; cool. Combine sugar, milk, and vanilla; stir into cooled chocolate mixture. Add more powdered sugar, if necessary, and stir until a smooth spreading consistency.

SWEET ENDINGS

Old-Fashioned German Potato Cake

1 cup butter (do not use margarine)	2 cups all-purpose flour
2 cups sugar	2 teaspoons baking powder
4 large eggs, separated	¼ teaspoon ground cinnamon
1 cup boiled and diced potatoes	¼ teaspoon ground cloves
½ cup grated chocolate	½ cup heavy whipping cream
1 cup chopped nuts	2-3 teaspoons grated lemon peel
	1 teaspoon vanilla extract

Cream butter; gradually add sugar, beating well at medium speed with an electric mixer. Add egg yolks, potatoes, chocolate and nuts, beating until well blended. Combine flour, baking powder, cinnamon and cloves; add to butter mixture alternately with cream. Stir in lemon peel and vanilla. Beat egg whites (at room temperature) in a large bowl until soft peaks form. Fold gently into batter. Pour into a greased 10-inch tube pan. Bake at 350 degrees for 1 hour or until a toothpick inserted in the center comes out clean. Cool in pan 10 minutes; remove from pan and let cool completely on a wire rack.

Yield: 12 to 16 servings

Note: 4 ounces melted chocolate may be substituted for grated chocolate.

Black Forest Cake

Cocoa powder	⅛ teaspoon salt
¾ cup vegetable oil	1 (21-ounce) can cherry pie filling
¾ cup sugar	1 (6-ounce) bag semisweet
2 large eggs	chocolate morsels
2 teaspoons vanilla extract	1 cup chopped walnuts
2 cups all-purpose flour	Garnishes: sifted powdered
1 teaspoon baking soda	sugar, cherries, whipped
1 teaspoon ground cinnamon	cream

Grease a 9-cup Bundt pan or 10-inch tube pan and dust with cocoa powder. Beat oil, sugar, eggs and vanilla in a mixing bowl at medium speed with an electric mixer. Combine flour, baking soda, cinnamon and salt; add to oil mixture, mixing well. Stir in pie filling, chocolate morsels and nuts. Pour into prepared pan. Bake at 350 degrees for 1 hour or until a wooden pick inserted in the center comes out clean. Cool in pan 10 minutes; remove from pan, and let cool completely on a wire rack. Sprinkle with powdered sugar and serve with additional cherries and whipped cream.

Yield: 12 servings

SWEET ENDINGS

Carrot Cake

2 cups all-purpose flour	2 cups finely grated carrots
2 cups sugar	1 teaspoon vanilla extract
2 teaspoons ground cinnamon	1 cup crushed pineapple, well
1 teaspoon baking powder	drained
½ teaspoon salt	1 cup shredded coconut
1 ½ cups vegetable oil	1 cup chopped nuts, divided
3 large eggs, lightly beaten	Cream Cheese Frosting

Combine flour, sugar, cinnamon, baking powder and salt in a large bowl. Stir in oil, eggs, carrots and vanilla, beating until well blended. Stir in pineapple, coconut and ½ cup nuts. Pour into a greased 13 x 9 x 2-inch baking pan. Bake at 350 degrees for 50 to 60 minutes. Cool completely on a wire rack. Spread Cream Cheese Frosting over top of cake. Sprinkle with remaining ½ cup nuts.

Yield: 12 to 16 servings

Cream Cheese Frosting:

6 tablespoons butter, softened	3 cups sifted powdered sugar
6 ounces cream cheese, softened	1 teaspoon vanilla extract

Beat butter and cream cheese at medium speed with an electric mixer until creamy; gradually add sugar at low speed until blended. Stir in vanilla. Beat at high speed to desired consistency. Cover and refrigerate until ready to use.

Oatmeal-Date Cake

This cake is better at least a day old.

1 cup quick-cooking oats	1 ½ cups flour
1 ½ cups boiling water	1 teaspoon baking soda
½ cup shortening	1 teaspoon salt
1 cup sugar	1 cup chopped dates
1 cup firmly packed light brown sugar	1 cup chopped nuts
2 large eggs	Coconut Frosting

Combine oats and boiling water in a small bowl; let stand for 20 minutes. Cream shortening; gradually add sugars, beating well at medium speed with an electric mixer. Add eggs, one at a time, beating well after each addition. Combine flour, baking soda and salt; add to shortening mixture alternately with oatmeal mixture, beating well. Stir in dates and nuts. Pour into a greased and floured 13 x 9 x 2-inch baking pan. Bake at 350 degrees for 35 to 40 minutes. Spread Coconut Frosting on top of warm cake. Broil top of cake for a few minutes until coconut is golden brown.

Coconut Frosting:

½ cup butter	1 teaspoon vanilla extract
½ cup firmly packed light brown sugar	1 cup flaked coconut
¼ cup heavy whipping cream	1 cup chopped nuts

Cream butter; gradually add sugar, beating at medium speed with an electric mixer. Beat in cream and vanilla. Stir in coconut and chopped nuts.

Yield: about 3 cups

Ravani (Greek Sponge Cake)

6	large eggs	2	teaspoons baking powder
1	cup farina (or Cream of Wheat)	1	cup butter, melted
1	cup all-purpose flour	3	cups water
3½	cups sugar, divided	1	cinnamon stick
2	tablespoons grated orange peel	¼	teaspoon lemon juice
1	teaspoon orange juice		Cherries, cut in half (optional)
			Finely chopped nuts (optional)

Beat eggs at high speed with an electric mixer until frothy. Add farina, flour, 1 cup sugar, orange peel, orange juice and baking powder, beating well. Stir in melted butter. Pour into a greased and floured 13 x 9 x 2-inch baking pan. Bake at 350 degrees for 25 to 30 minutes or until cake springs back when lightly touched. Combine remaining 2½ cups sugar, water and cinnamon in a saucepan over medium-high heat. Bring to a boil and stir in lemon juice. Reduce heat and simmer while cake bakes. Pour some syrup over the cake with a soup ladle. Cut cake into 4 lengthwise sections. Pour more syrup over cake. Cut diagonally into 1½-inch diamonds or squares; pour remaining syrup over cake. Place a cherry half on each piece or sprinkle with nuts. Cover and refrigerate 8 hours or overnight.

Yield: 16 to 20 servings

Chocolate Zucchini Cake

½	cup milk	¼	cup cocoa powder
1	teaspoon lemon juice	1	teaspoon baking soda
½	cup butter or margarine, softened	½	teaspoon baking powder
½	cup vegetable oil	½	teaspoon ground cinnamon
1¾	cups sugar	½	teaspoon ground cloves
2	large eggs	¼	cup semisweet chocolate morsels
1	teaspoon vanilla extract	2	cups finely diced zucchini (not shredded)
2½	cups all-purpose flour		

Combine milk and lemon juice in a small bowl; let stand 5 minutes. Cream butter and oil; gradually add sugar, beating well at medium speed with an electric mixer. Add eggs, vanilla and milk mixture, beating well. Combine flour, cocoa, baking powder, baking soda, cinnamon and cloves; add to butter mixture, beating well. Stir in zucchini. Spoon batter into a greased and floured 13 x 9 x 2-inch baking pan; sprinkle with chocolate morsels. Bake at 325 degrees for 40 to 45 minutes or until a toothpick inserted in the center comes out clean.

Yield: 15 servings

Hummingbird Cake

2	cups sugar	3	large eggs, lightly beaten
1	cup vegetable oil	3	cups all-purpose flour
1	(8-ounce) can crushed pineapple, drained	1	teaspoon salt
		1	teaspoon ground cinnamon
2	cups mashed bananas	1	cup chopped nuts
1 ½	teaspoons vanilla extract		Cream Cheese Frosting

Combine sugar, oil, pineapple, bananas, vanilla and eggs in a large bowl, blending well. Combine flour, salt, cinnamon and nuts; stir into egg mixture. Pour into a greased and floured 10-inch tube pan. Bake at 350 degrees for 1 hour 10 minutes or until a toothpick inserted in the center comes out clean. Cool in pan on a wire rack. Frost top and sides with Cream Cheese Frosting.

Yield: 12 to 16 servings

Cream Cheese Frosting:

¼	cup butter or margarine, softened	½	(16-ounce) box powdered sugar
½	(8-ounce) package cream cheese, softened	½	teaspoon vanilla extract

Beat together butter and cream cheese until creamy. Stir in powdered sugar and vanilla and beat until a smooth spreading consistency.

SWEET ENDINGS

Texas Sheet Cake

Chocolate lovers love this cake.

2	cups sugar	1	cup water
2	cups all-purpose flour	2	large eggs, lightly beaten
¼	cup cocoa	1	teaspoon baking soda
½	cup milk	1	teaspoon vanilla extract
2	teaspoons vinegar		Cocoa Frosting
1	cup butter or margarine		

Combine sugar, flour and cocoa in a large mixing bowl; set aside. Combine milk and vinegar in a saucepan. Add butter and water. Bring mixture to a boil, stirring until butter melts. Stir into flour mixture; cool slightly. Add eggs, baking soda and vanilla, stirring until well blended. (Batter will be thin.) Pour into a greased 15 x 10-inch jelly-roll pan. Bake at 400 degrees for 15 minutes; cool slightly. Spread Cocoa Frosting over very warm cake.

Yield: 18 servings

Cocoa Frosting:

½	cup butter or margarine	¼	cup cocoa powder
6	tablespoons milk	1	teaspoon vanilla extract
1	(16-ounce) box powdered sugar		

Combine butter and milk in a saucepan over medium-high heat, stirring until butter melts. Bring mixture to a boil. Remove from heat and stir in powdered sugar, cocoa and vanilla.

SWEET ENDINGS

Raspberry Truffle Cake

16 (1-ounce) squares semisweet chocolate, chopped
½ cup butter
1 tablespoon sugar
1½ teaspoons all-purpose flour
1 teaspoon raspberry liqueur (optional)

4 large eggs, separated
1 (12-ounce) jar seedless raspberry jam (1 cup)
Whipped cream
Fresh raspberries

Combine chocolate and butter in a large, heavy saucepan over low heat. Cook, stirring constantly, until mixture is smooth. Remove from heat. Stir in sugar, flour and liqueur. Beat egg yolks into mixture with a wooden spoon, one at a time, until well blended. Set aside. Beat egg whites (at room temperature) in a mixing bowl on high speed until stiff peaks form. Fold into chocolate mixture. Pour into a greased 8-inch springform pan. Bake at 350 degrees for 25 to 30 minutes or until edges puff. Cool on a wire rack for 30 minutes. Remove sides of pan; cool completely. Cover and refrigerate for 4 to 24 hours. Heat jam until just melted. To serve, drizzle jam on each plate and top with a cake slice, whipped cream and fresh raspberries.

Yield: 12 servings

Southern Peanut Butter Pie

1	cup powdered sugar	⅛	teaspoon salt
½	cup peanut butter	2	tablespoons butter
2	cups milk	1	teaspoon vanilla extract
3	egg yolks	1	(9-inch) unbaked pie shell
⅓	cup sugar	1	cup heavy whipping cream,
¼	cup cornstarch		whipped and sweetened

Combine powdered sugar and peanut butter in a small bowl, mixing well; set aside. Place milk in top of a double boiler; bring water to a boil. Cook until milk is thoroughly heated. Set aside.

Beat egg yolks at medium speed with an electric mixer until frothy. Add sugar, cornstarch and salt; beat until thick. Gradually stir about 1 cup hot milk into yolk mixture; add to remaining milk, stirring constantly. Cook mixture in the double boiler over low heat, stirring constantly, until mixture is smooth and thick. Remove from heat; add butter and vanilla, stirring until butter melts. Cover the bottom of the pie shell with two-thirds of the peanut butter mixture. Pour the custard over the peanut butter mixture; cool. Combine remaining peanut butter mixture and whipped cream in a bowl and spread over cooled pie.

Yield: 6 to 8 servings

Who wants to make pies like Mother makes when it's so much simpler to let Mother make them in the first place?

SWEET ENDINGS

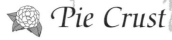 *Pie Crust*

1 (5-pound) bag all-purpose flour	1 (3-pound) container shortening
2 tablespoons salt	½ cup light corn syrup
	3 cups cold water

Combine flour and salt in a very large bowl; cut in shortening with a pastry blender or fork until mixture resembles a coarse meal. Combine syrup and 1½ cups water in a bowl, stirring to blend. Stir in remaining 1½ cups water. Sprinkle syrup mixture evenly over flour mixture; stir until dry ingredients are moistened (you may have to use your hands). Divide into balls the size of a large orange. Place each ball in a plastic freezer bag; flatten ball into disk. Repeat with remaining dough. Place in the freezer until ready to use. Thaw pastry disks at room temperature and roll on a lightly floured surface to fit pie pan.

Yield: about 21 crusts

For flakier crust on fruit pies, always bake in a glass, ovenproof pan on the lowest oven shelf. Or, sprinkle a combination of sugar and flour on the lower crust before putting in the filling.

 *Swedish Apple Pie*

½ cup sugar	1 large egg, lightly beaten
½ cup all-purpose flour	1 teaspoon vanilla extract
1 teaspoon baking powder	1 cup peeled and chopped
Dash salt	apple

Combine sugar, flour, baking powder, salt in a bowl. Stir in egg, vanilla and apple. Spoon into a greased 8- or 9-inch pie plate. Bake at 350 degrees for 25 to 30 minutes. Serve warm with whipped cream or ice cream.

SWEET ENDINGS

Orange Velvet Pie

1 (3-ounce) package orange-flavored gelatin	¼ cup orange juice
1 cup hot water	1 teaspoon lemon juice
1 (8-ounce) package Neufchâtel cheese	1 cup heavy whipping cream, whipped
¼ cup sugar	1 (9-inch) baked pie shell or graham cracker crust

Dissolve gelatin in hot water; set aside. Beat cream cheese at high speed with an electric mixer until smooth. Add sugar, orange juice and lemon juice, beating until well blended. Gradually beat in gelatin mixture. Cover and refrigerate until almost set. Beat whipped cream into gelatin mixture; pour into pie shell. Cover and refrigerate until firm.

Yield: 1 (9-inch) pie

Note: 1 (1.3-ounce) envelope whipped dairy topping, prepared according to package directions may be substituted for whipped cream.

Pecan-Pumpkin Pie

This pie is not as sweet as most pecan pies.

3 large eggs	1 teaspoon vanilla extract
½ cup firmly packed light brown sugar	¼ cup butter or margarine, melted
1 cup light corn syrup	1 cup pecans
½ cup canned pumpkin	1 (9-inch) unbaked pie shell
¼ teaspoon salt	

Beat together eggs, sugar, syrup, pumpkin, salt and vanilla in a large mixing bowl with an electric mixer. Stir in butter and pecans. Pour into pie shell. Bake at 375 degrees for 45 minutes or until set. Serve warm or cold.

Yield: 6 to 8 servings

SWEET ENDINGS

Grandma's Apple Pie

"Apple pie without cheese is like a kiss without a squeeze"
—a direct quote from my grandmother.

2 ¼ cups all-purpose flour, divided	2 tablespoons butter, melted
1 ½ teaspoons salt, divided	3 tablespoons ground cinnamon
¾ cup shortening	½ teaspoon nutmeg
5 tablespoons ice water	Sugar
6 cups peeled and sliced apples	Cheddar cheese
1 cup sugar	

Combine 2 cups flour and 1 teaspoon salt; cut in shortening with a pastry blender or fork until mixture resembles a coarse meal. Sprinkle ice water, 1 tablespoon at a time, evenly over surface; stir with a fork until mixture holds together. Roll out two-thirds of the dough on a lightly floured surface to line a 9-inch pie pan; set aside remaining dough. Combine apples, sugar, butter, remaining ¼ cup flour, remaining ½ teaspoon salt, cinnamon and nutmeg in a large bowl, blending well. Pour into prepared crust. Roll and cut remaining dough into strips and arrange on top of pie to form a lattice crust. Sprinkle with sugar. Bake at 375 degrees for 1 hour. Serve warm or cold with sliced cheddar cheese.

Yield: 1 (9-inch) pie

Sour Cream Raisin Pie

2 large eggs	1 teaspoon ground cinnamon
1 ½ cups sour cream	1 teaspoon ground cloves
1 cup sugar	1 cup raisins
2 tablespoons all-purpose flour	1 (9-inch) unbaked pie shell

Combine eggs, sour cream, sugar, flour, cinnamon and cloves in a large mixing bowl; beat at medium speed with an electric mixer until well blended. Stir in raisins. Pour into pie shell. Bake at 400 degrees for 10 minutes. Reduce heat to 350 degrees and bake for 30 minutes or until set.

Yield: 6 to 8 servings

Light Pumpkin Pie

⅔ cup sugar	1 ½ cups canned pumpkin
½ teaspoon salt	1 ½ cups evaporated skim milk
½ teaspoon ground cinnamon	1 teaspoon vanilla extract
½ teaspoon ground ginger	½ teaspoon grated orange peel
½ teaspoon nutmeg	3 egg whites, lightly beaten
Pinch ground cloves	1 (9-inch) unbaked pie shell

Combine sugar, salt, cinnamon, ginger, nutmeg and cloves in a large mixing bowl. Stir in pumpkin. Add milk, vanilla, orange peel and egg whites; beat at medium speed with an electric mixer until smooth. Pour into pie shell and place on lowest rack in oven. Bake at 450 degrees for 10 minutes; reduce heat to 325 and bake 45 minutes or until a knife inserted in the center comes out clean.

Yield: 8 servings at 210 calories each or 10 servings at 165 calories each

Walnut Pie

1 cup sugar	1 cup graham cracker crumbs
3 large eggs	¾ cup chopped walnuts
½ teaspoon vanilla extract	

Combine sugar and eggs, beating at medium speed with an electric mixer until well blended. Stir in vanilla, graham cracker crumbs and walnuts. Pour into a greased and floured 9-inch pie pan. Bake at 350 degrees for 20 to 25 minutes. Serve with whipped cream or ice cream.

Yield: 1 (9-inch) pie

Store nuts in the refrigerator or freezer so they won't become rancid.

SWEET ENDINGS

Sour Cream Lemon Pie

"The best-ever lemon pie!"

1 cup sugar	1 cup light cream
3 tablespoons cornstarch	¼ cup butter
1 tablespoon all-purpose flour	1 cup sour cream
1 tablespoon grated lemon peel	1 (9-inch) baked pie shell
⅓ cup fresh lemon juice	

Topping:

1 cup heavy whipping cream	Garnishes: lemon slices,
2 tablespoons powdered sugar	grated lemon peel, fresh
½ cup sour cream	mint sprigs
½ teaspoon almond extract	

Combine sugar, cornstarch, flour, lemon peel, lemon juice and cream in a saucepan over medium heat. Bring mixture to a boil, stirring constantly. Add butter and cook, stirring constantly, until thick and smooth. Remove from heat; let cool. Stir in sour cream and pour into pie shell. Refrigerate until ready to serve.

Beat whipping cream until foamy; gradually add powdered sugar, beating until soft peaks form. Fold in sour cream and almond extract. Spread topping over pie. Garnish with lemon slices, lemon peel and fresh mint.

Yield: 1 (9-inch) pie

Microwave lemons for 25 seconds for more juice.

SWEET ENDINGS

Tangy Lemon Pie

½	cup butter, melted	½	cup fresh lemon juice
2	cups sugar	1	(8-inch) deep dish pie shell,
4	large eggs, lightly beaten		unbaked
2	tablespoons grated lemon peel		

Combine butter, sugar, eggs, lemon peel and lemon juice in a bowl; stir until well blended. Pour into pie shell. Bake at 350 degrees for 30 to 40 minutes.

Yield: 6 to 8 servings

Note: you may use 2 regular pie shells, but the filling will be thin.

 One lemon yields about ¼ cup juice; one orange yields about ⅓ cup juice.

Butterscotch Pie

¼	cup butter or margarine	⅛	teaspoon salt
2	cups firmly packed dark	6	egg yolks, lightly beaten
	brown sugar	3	cups milk
2	tablespoons all-purpose flour	2	teaspoons vanilla extract
2	tablespoons cornstarch	1	(9-inch) baked pie shell

Melt butter in a large saucepan over medium heat. Stir in brown sugar, flour, cornstarch, salt, egg yolks and milk. Cook over medium heat, stirring constantly, until mixture is thickened and bubbly. Reduce heat and cook, stirring constantly, for 2 minutes. Remove from heat and stir in vanilla. Pour into pie shell. Cover and refrigerate several hours or overnight.

Yield: 8 servings

SWEET ENDINGS

Double Chocolate Silk Pie

1 ½ cups chocolate wafer crumbs
6 tablespoons butter, melted
1 ½ cups heavy cream
3 tablespoons sugar
5 egg yolks, lightly beaten

10 (1-ounce) squares semisweet
    chocolate, finely chopped
1 ½ teaspoon vanilla extract
    Garnishes: shaved chocolate
    scrolls, whipped cream

Combine crumbs and butter; press into the bottom and up sides of a 9-inch pie plate. Cover and refrigerate until ready to fill. Pour cream into the top of a double boiler; bring water to a boil. Reduce heat to low; add sugar, stirring until dissolved. Whisk ¼ cup of cream mixture into yolks. Pour yolk mixture into remaining cream mixture. Cook for 8 to 10 minutes, stirring constantly, until mixture coats the back of a spoon. Remove from heat; add chocolate and vanilla, stirring until well blended. Pour into prepared pie crust and cool to room temperature. Cover and refrigerate 8 hours or overnight. Garnish with shaved chocolate scrolls and whipped cream.

Key Lime Pie ✓

2 large eggs
2 egg whites
½ cup Key lime juice
1 teaspoon grated lime peel
1 (14-ounce) can fat-free
    sweetened condensed milk

1 (8-inch) graham cracker pie
    crust
    Whipped cream or whipped
    topping

Beat eggs and egg whites at medium speed with an electric mixer until well blended. Gradually add juice, peel and condensed milk, mixing well. Spoon mixture into crust. Bake at 350 degrees for 20 minutes or until almost set (the center will not be firm, but will set as it cools). Cool on a wire rack. Cover loosely and refrigerate 4 hours. Top with whipped cream.

Yield: 8 servings

SWEET ENDINGS

Sweet Potato Pecan Pie

2 cups cooked, mashed sweet potatoes	¼ teaspoon ground cinnamon
	¼ teaspoon maple flavoring
½ cup sugar	⅛ teaspoon ground ginger
½ cup firmly packed light brown sugar	4 large eggs
	1 cup chopped pecans
¼ teaspoon salt	1 (9-inch) unbaked pie shell

Combine potatoes, sugar, brown sugar, salt, cinnamon, maple flavoring and ginger in a large mixing bowl, mixing well. Add eggs, one at a time, beating well after each addition. Stir in pecans. Pour into pie shell. Bake at 375 degrees for 45 minutes. Reduce heat to 325 degrees and bake 11 minutes. Cool pie on wire rack.

Yield: 6 to 8 servings

Peach Praline Pie

4 cups sliced fresh peaches	¼ cup firmly packed light brown sugar
½ cup sugar	
2 tablespoons tapioca	½ cup chopped pecans
1 teaspoon lemon juice	¼ cup butter
½ cup all-purpose flour	1 (9-inch) unbaked pie shell

Combine peaches, sugar, tapioca and lemon juice in a large bowl; let stand for 15 minutes. Combine flour, brown sugar and pecans in a bowl; cut in butter with a pastry blender or fork until mixture resembles a coarse meal. Sprinkle one-third of pecan mixture in the bottom of pie shell. Top with peach mixture. Sprinkle remaining pecan mixture over peaches. Bake at 450 degrees for 10 minutes. Reduce heat to 350 degrees and bake 20 minutes. Cool on a wire rack. Serve at room temperature.

Yield: 6 to 8 servings

SWEET ENDINGS

Sweetheart Fudge Pie

½ cup butter or margarine, softened

¾ cup firmly packed light brown sugar

3 large eggs

1 (12-ounce) package semisweet chocolate morsels, melted

2 teaspoons instant coffee granules

1 teaspoon rum extract

½ cup all-purpose flour

1 cup coarsely chopped walnuts

1 (9-inch) unbaked pie shell

Garnish: whipped cream and chopped walnuts (optional)

Cream butter; gradually add brown sugar, beating at medium speed with an electric mixer until light and fluffy. Add eggs, one at a time, beating well after each addition. Add melted chocolate, coffee granules and rum extract; mix well. Stir in flour and walnuts. Pour into pie shell. Bake at 375 degrees for 25 minutes. Cool completely on a wire rack. Cover and refrigerate until well chilled. Garnish with whipped cream and walnuts, if desired.

Yield: 8 servings

The Island has benefited immeasurably by your caring project and continuing involvement in all aspects of our community. It has certainly helped us create a legacy of education at Coastal Discovery, The Museum on Hilton Head Island. We wouldn't be where we are without you.

 Keep baking chocolate in a cool, dry pantry for best storage.

Etcetera

Twice Treasured Recipes that shouldn't be left out . . . full of flavor and ready to be devoured by hungry hordes.

The final view is a sandy sun-dappled Low Country lane. Imagine a languorous stroll through semi-tropical woods, redolent with the delicate sweet fragrance of Yellow Jessamine, and the clean zesty scent of Pine. Lining the lane are Saw Palmettos with razor sharp spikes—sharp enough to slice leather—fanning from long stems. Further along a Rufous-Sided Towhee trills "drink-your-tea" from an aromatic Wax Myrtle, making you think of a tall cool glass of sweet tea. Squirrels scurry in moss-covered branches overhead, as a brilliant Painted Bunting flitters past in the distance. You may be quietly enjoying a friend's laugh as you contemplate the pleasures of a picnic to come at the end of the lane. Treasured memories . . . treasured friends . . . treasured family . . . these are the *Twice Treasured Recipes* to share with your loved ones.

Etcetera

Etcetera

Quick and Easy Recipes are designated with a camellia flower.
Memorable Menu Recipes are designated with a leaf.

ETCETERA

 # Cocktail Sauce

6 ounces (about ¾ cup) chili sauce	½ teaspoon Worcestershire sauce
6 ounces (about ¾ cup) ketchup	¼ teaspoon celery salt
1 tablespoon lemon juice	Dash pepper
1 tablespoon prepared horseradish	

Combine all ingredients, mixing well. Add an additional scant teaspoon of horseradish for spicier sauce.

Yield: 1 ½ cups

 # Lemon Cocktail Sauce

6 tablespoons mayonnaise	1 teaspoon prepared mustard
2 tablespoons lemon juice	½ teaspoon grated onion
1 tablespoons horseradish sauce	

Combine all ingredients, mixing well. Good on seafood, asparagus, artichokes or broccoli.

Yield: ½ cup

Some say that too many cooks will spoil the broth, but I like help.

Flank Steak Marinade

¼ cup dry sherry
¼ cup low-sodium soy sauce
¼ cup honey
2 tablespoons white wine vinegar

1 tablespoons peeled and minced fresh ginger
1 teaspoon dark sesame oil
2 cloves garlic, crushed

Combine all ingredients, mixing well.

Yield: 1 cup

Tangy Marinade for Beef or Chicken

½ cup vegetable oil
½ cup soy sauce
⅓ cup vinegar
¼ cup chopped onion
1 tablespoon chopped fresh parsley

1 tablespoon dry mustard
2 cloves garlic, minced
1 teaspoon freshly ground pepper
Salt

Combine all ingredients, mixing well.

Yield: 2½ cups

Ripe Olive Chop-Chop ✓

This is a delicious accompaniment for most stews, especially lamb.

3	(2 ½-ounce) cans chopped ripe olives	1	clove garlic, minced
1 ½	cups finely chopped celery	1	(2-ounce) can anchovy fillets
1	cup finely chopped dill pickle (about 4 medium)	½	cup vegetable or olive oil
½	cup finely sliced green onions	¼	cup wine or apple cider vinegar
		¼	teaspoon pepper

Combine olives, celery, pickle, green onion and garlic in a large bowl; toss lightly to mix. Drain oil from anchovies into olive mixture; chop anchovies into tiny pieces. Stir anchovies, oil, vinegar and pepper into the olive mixture, tossing well to mix. Cover and refrigerate several hours or overnight.

Yield: 2 cups

Quick Italian Tomato Sauce

2	tablespoons olive oil	½	cup brewed coffee
½	cup chopped onion	1	teaspoon salt
1	clove garlic, minced	⅛	teaspoon pepper
1	pound lean ground beef	½	cup canned, sliced mushrooms, drained
1	(11-ounce) can tomato soup	¼	teaspoon dried oregano
2	(6-ounce) cans tomato paste		

Heat oil in a large skillet over medium-high heat. Add onion and garlic; sauté until golden brown. Stir in beef; cook until mixture crumbles; drain if desired. Stir in soup, paste, coffee, salt and pepper. Bring mixture to a boil, reduce heat to very low, and simmer 30 minutes or until thick. Stir in mushrooms and oregano; simmer 5 to 10 minutes, adding ½ cup water if necessary.

Yield: 6 servings

ETCETERA

 # Dipping Sauce for Vegetables

⅓ cup mayonnaise	1 tablespoon ketchup
¼ cup chili sauce	2 teaspoons Worcestershire
2½ tablespoons prepared	sauce
horseradish	1 teaspoon steak sauce

Combine ingredients, whisking until smooth.

Yield: 1½ cups

 # Fruit Salsa

1 cup diced mango or	1 cup diced pineapple
cantaloupe	¼ cup coconut rum
1 cup diced papaya	2 tablespoons sugar

Combine all ingredients in a medium bowl, mixing well.

¼ cup pineapple juice and ½ teaspoon rum extract may be substituted for rum.

Yield: 10 servings

Cranberry Relish

1 (16-ounce) can whole-berry	1 (8-ounce) can crushed
cranberry sauce	pineapple, undrained
1 (11-ounce) can Mandarin	1 cup chopped walnuts
orange segments, drained	

Combine all ingredients in a medium bowl, mixing well. Cover and chill until serving.

Yield: about 3½ cups

ETCETERA

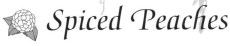

Spiced Peaches √

½ cup sugar
½ cup peach juice
¼ cup vinegar

⅓ cup red hot cinnamon candy
    or 8 to 10 whole cloves and
    1 stick cinnamon
1 (14.5-ounce) can peach halves

Combine sugar, juice, vinegar, and seasoning in a saucepan over medium-high heat. Bring to a boil, reduce heat, and simmer 10 minutes. Stir in fruit; cook until thoroughly heated. Place mixture in a shallow container; cover and refrigerate 8 hours or overnight.

Yield: 2 ½ cups

Sugar Coated Peanuts

1 cup sugar
½ cup water

2 cups raw, shelled peanuts
    (skin on)

Combine sugar and water in a saucepan over medium heat. Add peanuts and cook, stirring frequently, until peanuts are completely sugared and liquid is gone. Pour peanuts evenly on an ungreased baking sheet. Bake at 300 degrees for 30 minutes, stirring every 5 minutes.

Yield: 2 cups

Add a dash of nutmeg to a white sauce for great taste.

ETCETERA

 # Spiced Pecans

1 egg white	1 teaspoon ground cinnamon
1 tablespoon water	½ teaspoon salt
3 cups pecan halves	½ teaspoon ground cloves
½ cup sugar	½ teaspoon ground nutmeg

Beat egg white and water in a large bowl. Add pecans, stirring until all surfaces are moistened. Combine sugar, cinnamon, salt, cloves and nutmeg; sprinkle over pecans, mixing well. Spread pecans on a foil-lined baking sheet. Bake at 300 degrees for 30 minutes, stirring every 10 minutes. Remove from oven; dry pecans in a single layer.

Yield: 3 cups

 # Kahlúa Fudge Topping

1 cup cocoa powder	1 cup heavy whipping cream
⅔ cup sugar	½ cup butter, melted
½ cup firmly packed light brown sugar	¼ cup Kahlúa
	1 ⅓ teaspoons vanilla extract

Combine cocoa, sugar and light brown sugar in a heavy saucepan over medium heat, stirring well. Stir in cream, butter and Kahlúa. Bring mixture to a boil; boil 1 minute, stirring constantly. Remove from heat; stir in vanilla. Store in a covered jar in the refrigerator. Serve warm or at room temperature over ice cream or layered in a parfait.

Yield: 2¾ cups

 Toasting nuts, such as walnuts and pecans, brings out the flavor and restores crispness. Spread nuts on a baking sheet and bake at 325 degrees for 5 to 15 minutes.

ETCETERA

 # Dixie Chocolate Sauce

⅓ cup sugar
¼ cup water
1 tablespoon light corn syrup
1 (1-ounce) square unsweetened
   chocolate, chopped

Dash salt
¼ cup peanut butter
¼ teaspoon vanilla extract

Combine sugar, water, syrup, chocolate and salt in a heavy saucepan. Bring mixture to a boil, stirring constantly until sugar dissolves and chocolate melts. Reduce heat to low and simmer for 3 minutes. Remove from heat and stir in peanut butter and vanilla. Serve hot over ice cream.

Yield: ¾ cup

 # Two-Minute Velvet Fudge

3 cups (18 ounces) semisweet
   chocolate morsels
1 (14-ounce) can sweetened
   condensed milk

⅓ cup powdered sugar
2 teaspoons vanilla extract
1 cup chopped walnuts

Microwave: Place morsels and condensed milk in a 2-quart microwave-safe bowl. Microwave on HIGH for 2 minutes; stir until smooth. Stir in sugar, vanilla and walnuts, mixing well. Pour into a greased 8 x 8-inch baking pan. Refrigerate 1½ hours or until firm. Cut into 16, 2-inch squares. Store tightly covered in a cool place for up to 2 weeks.

Rangetop: Place morsels and condensed milk in a 2-quart saucepan over medium heat. Cook 8 minutes, stirring often, until chocolate melts and mixture is smooth. Remove from heat; stir in sugar, vanilla and walnuts, mixing well. Pour into a greased 8 x 8-inch baking pan. Refrigerate 1½ hours or until firm. Cut into 16, 2-inch squares. Store tightly covered in a cool place for up to 2 weeks.

Yield: 16 (2-inch) squares

ETCETERA

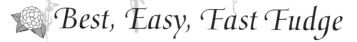

Best, Easy, Fast Fudge

1	(16-ounce) package powdered sugar	¼	teaspoon salt
½	cup cocoa powder	¼	teaspoon ground cinnamon
¼	cup milk	½	cup butter, cut into pieces
1	tablespoon vanilla extract	1	cup chopped pecans

Line bottom of an 8 x 8-inch baking pan with wax paper; set aside. Combine sugar, cocoa, milk, vanilla, salt and cinnamon in a 2-quart microwave-safe baking dish, stirring gently. Top with butter. Microwave, uncovered on HIGH for 3 minutes or until heated. Stir until smooth; stir in pecans. Pour into prepared pan; refrigerate 1 ½ hours or until firm. Cut into 16, 2-inch squares. Store tightly covered in a cool place for up to 2 weeks.

Yield: 16 (2-inch) squares

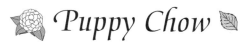

Puppy Chow

It really does look like Puppy Chow, but it's too tasty for dogs!

½	cup butter or margarine	1	(12-ounce) box crisp rice cereal squares
1	(12-ounce) bag semisweet chocolate morsels	2	cups powdered sugar
½	cup creamy peanut butter		

Combine butter, morsels and peanut butter in a heavy saucepan over low heat. Cook until melted, stirring to blend. Place cereal in a large bowl; pour chocolate mixture over cereal, tossing to coat. Pour coated cereal and powdered sugar in a brown grocery bag; shake until well coated. You can substitute 1 cup butterscotch morsels and 1 cup semisweet morsels for the 12-ounce bag of semisweet morsels.

ETCETERA

Crazy Crunch

2 quarts popped corn
1 ½ cups pecan pieces
⅔ cup almonds
1 ⅓ cups sugar

1 cup butter or margarine
½ cup light corn syrup
1 teaspoon vanilla extract

Combine popped corn, pecans and almonds on a baking sheet. Combine sugar, butter and syrup in a 1 ½-quart saucepan over medium heat. Bring mixture to a boil; boil, stirring occasionally, for 10 to 15 minutes or until mixture turns a light caramel color. Remove from heat. Stir in vanilla. Pour over nut mixture, tossing to coat. Spread mixture out evenly to dry. Break apart clumps. Store in tightly covered containers.

Yield: 2 pounds

Cheddar Dumplings

1 ½ cups self-rising flour
½ teaspoon dry mustard
½ cup shortening

½ (2 ounces) shredded cheddar cheese
⅔ cup milk

Combine flour and dry mustard in a medium bowl; cut in shortening with a pastry blender or fork until crumbly. Stir in cheese and milk. Drop by spoonfuls into simmering soups or stews. Cook, covered, for 10 to 15 minutes until dumplings are firm.

 For free-flowing salt, add a few grains of raw rice to the salt shaker. Vital information for a humid climate.

Afterword

We gratefully acknowledge all of our volunteers who generously shared their kitchens, recipes, artistic and literary talents, time and ideas. You've made the dream become a reality.

We are grateful to each recipe contributor who donated recipes for use in *Twice Treasured Recipes*.

Unfortunately, duplication of recipes and lack of space prevented us from incorporating *all* the treasured recipes submitted. We sincerely hope that no one's name has been unintentionally omitted.

May our twice treasured collection of regional favorites warm the hearths and hearts of every kitchen it reaches.

Helen Abbott
Ben Baldwin
Jeanne Baldwin
Toni Barner
Mary Batastini
Sally Baxter
Kay Berger
Shirley Beadling
Patty Billman
Bluffton Self Help, Inc.
Martha Bolton
Newell Bolton
Bea Boyd
Leah Bratt
Elaine Brazer
Rosemarie Brill
Rosemary Brisendine
Connie Brooks
Jerry Brown

Roosevelt Brownlee, Jr.
Greg Burnham
Betty Bush
Carolyn Butler
Carole Calder
Alice Camp
Barbara Canham
Betsy Catlin
Susan Cato, Executive Director of CAPA Child Abuse Prevention Center
Mary Jane Chapman
Wilhelmina Chaplin of The Penn Center
Lois Claus
Coastal Discovery, The Museum on Hilton Head
Jane Conklin

Leslie Cosacchi
Anne Coulter
Crowne Plaza Resorts
Gloria Daly, Executive Director of the Hilton Head Orchestra
Ruth Doig
Evie Huebler-Dolbey
Susan Dorn
Betsy Doughtie, Director of Deep Well
Emmy Drylie
Dot Duncan
Leigh Fadden
Miriam Farmer
Janet Fischer
Gayle Fisher
Nancy Fisher
Harriet Gallow
Annette Gilbert

Margaret Gough
Earlene Graudin
Stuart Gregg
Wini Gregg
Mary Grindstaff
Michelle Harmon
Millie Haskell
Lois Heitzke
June Hendricks
Maryjean Herberger
Bette Herbig
Marge Huck
Hyatt of Hilton Head
John Jakes
Willie May Jones
Jean Kaley
Sally Kidd
Gussie Kimbrough
Fran Kilmar
Dottie Kochli
Nina Landry
Mel Langan
Eleanor Lehman
Betty Lewis
Celeste Lister
Helen Luecke
Jeanne MacVicar
Walter R. Mack of The
   Penn Center
Roberta Mattka
Lottie McCowan

Lisa McCoy
Joanne McCreight
John McCreight
Jeanne McVicar
Lyn Meachen
Evelyn Mitchell
Mina Mulrain
Terry Murphy
Pat Nelson
Karen Ostby
Jane Ostergard
Lois Petersen
Chris Tenne Pendleton
Doris Pinkham
Madeline Perry
Barb Plank
Ange Ploussard
Roger Reynolds
Lois Riddell
Mary Ann Root
Rita Rosen
Shirley Rowe
Pat Russell
Rosa G. Simons of
   The Penn Center
Sally Schubert
Terry Sechrist
Frank Selvy
Liz Seymour
Joyce Siebers
June Shaw

Stan Smith
Kit Steffen
Marge Strickland
Carol Toti
Dot Thompson
Lois Thompson
Ann Ulrich
Janet VanTrigt
Linda Vingelen
Charlotte Ward
Marty Waltz
Betty Wasson
Gov. John West
Doris Woods
Edna Wilcher
Joan Wilson
Rosie Wilson

NOTES

INDEX

INDEX

INDEX

278

INDEX

INDEX

INDEX

INDEX

INDEX

INDEX

INDEX

INDEX

INDEX